The Complete Book of Casting

The Complete Book of Casting

REX GERLACH

with photographs by the author

Winchester Press

Library of Congress Catalog Card Number: 74-16869
ISBN: 0-87691-163-7

Published by Winchester Press
205 E. 42nd St., New York, N.Y. 10017

Printed in the United States of America

To my beloved wife,
Joanie,
whose patience, understanding, and assistance
made this book possible.

Acknowledgments

The author wishes to acknowledge the kind assistance of the following persons and firms in helping to compile the historical and technical chapters of this work:

Mr. Richard C. Wolff, Vice-President, Garcia Corporation; Mr. Phil Clock, President, Fenwick/Sevenstrand; Mr. Kenny Kawakami, Executive Vice-President, Daiwa Corp.; Mr. Bill Laurent, Shakespeare Sporting Goods Division; Mr. John Sweeney, Wright & McGill Co.; Mr. Jack Macken, Newton Line Company; Mr. Tony Skilton, Orvis Company; Mr. George Pandaleon, Martin Reel Co.; Mr. John R. Powers, Jr., Daisy & Heddon Divisions, Victor Comptometer Corp.; Mr. R. F. Jennings, Cortland Line Company; Mr. Vern Buchman, Berkley & Company, Inc.; Mr. T. David Zeigler, Browning; Mr. Richard Bear, Bear Advertising; Mr. Fred A. Greenwood, Plastics Department, E. I. du Pont de Nemours & Company; Mr. Tom Prather, James Heddon's Sons; Mr. H. A. Ashby, Conolon; Mr. Paul A. Mulready, Vice-President/General Manager, Johnson Reels Company; Mrs. Margaret Riggs, Shakespeare Sporting Goods Division; Mr. Stephen K. Peterson, Wright & McGill Co.; Mr. Robert L. Pigg; Mr. Michael M. Stocker, President, California Tackle Company; and the American Casting Association.

The author's special thanks go to Mr. Lew Jewett of the Leisure Time Products New Business Ventures Division, 3M Company; and to Mr. Leon L. Martuch of Scientific Anglers/3M for their coordinative efforts that made certain of the casting sequences possible and for providing special arc-white lines and rods to enhance the quality of the casting photos.

The author's special thanks go also to the fine casters who assisted in producing the actual rapid-sequence photos, including Mr. William Frazer, Sales Manager, Scientific Anglers/3M; M/Sgt. Thomas H. Stouffer, USAF (ret.); Mr. Hardy Kruse; Mr. Milton Kahl; Mr. Gil Hokanson; and Mr. Larry Dahlberg.

My sincere thanks go also to the technical experts who helped so materially in preparing the chapter on rod and casting dynamics, including Mr. Cecil E. Jacobs, laboratory supervisor of 3M's Leisure Time Products New Business Ventures Division; Mr. Michael M. Stocker, California Tackle Company; Mr. Leon L. Martuch, Scientific Anglers/3M; and Dr. James Imai, University of California at Domingues Hills.

A special note of thanks is also extended to Mr. Ray N. Smith of Saginaw, Michigan, for his most generous hospitality while the author was shooting certain casting sequences in that area, and to the members of the Pasadena Casting Club, Pasadena, California, for the use of their fine facilities while photographing the long-leader casting sequences.

Contents

The Complete Book of Casting

Chapter 1

The Basis of Modern Casting

Present-day casting methods have evolved down through the very distinct ages of sport-fishing as a result of certain milestone achievements in tackle-making technology and the concerted efforts of anglers of the times to take full advantage of them. Casting's metamorphosis was a slow one, at times almost glacial in pace—until the mid-1800s, that is. In the wake of the industrial revolution both here and abroad, tackle manufacture got on a downhill track, and for the last three decades, technological advances have come about so rapidly that it has been virtually impossible for the average casting angler to keep on top of them all.

In order to understand more fully how casting had its beginnings and how incredibly far it has come in recent years, let's start where the sport of angling had its beginnings—in the ancient lands of the Middle and Far East.

The Ancients

Early paintings by Chinese, Egyptians, and Assyrians clearly indicate that fishing was practiced at least 5,000 years ago. Historians say the Chinese began to fish about 900 B.C. and that they were the first people to employ lines braided from silk. The Jews started fishing about the fifth century B.C. and are credited with introducing the woven net, which stimulated a then-brand-new commercial endeavor—wholesale fishing. The Romans were also skilled fishermen and possibly the first to use artificial lures shaped like fish.

Although Martial is credited by some to have been the first to write about fly-fishing during the first two decades following the birth of Christ, it's more likely that Claudius Aelian (230–170 B.C.)

deserves the credit. He described a Macedonian method of fishing with a crude form of artificial fly fashioned out of red wool and a wax-colored cock's feather. Aelian noted that the Macedonian fishing rod was some 6 feet long and that the line was of similar length. Fishing reels were unknown in those times. The line was attached directly to the tip of the rod.

There is no really reliable evidence to date precisely when the first fishing rod came into being, nor when it was first used for purely sporting purposes, but the 5,000-year-old paintings mentioned above show rods in use.

Two millennia later, Homer wrote of Scylla as "being an angler . . . who with a long rod casts his ox-horn lure into the sea." And we know that by Cleopatra's time, fishing was a well-established form of recreation.

It may well be that Aelian's words were the first historical reference to fly-casting as such. He said that the fly was thrown in the direction of the fish. However, it's likely that the method of presentation was a *dapping* of the fly on the water to attract the salmonids that were their quarry.

The Early English Writers

Although there was no apparent lack of angling activity during the centuries following Aelian's commentary, little significant literature was written on the subject from which to form a clear mental picture of the equipment and techniques used in those times.

It wasn't until 1486 that the Abbess of Sopwell, Dame Juliana de Berners, wrote her now famous *A Treatyse of Fysshynge Wyth an Angle,* the first English-language book on fishing, in which she described a fly bearing striking similarity to those used by the early Macedonians.

Another two centuries sped by before any other really significant books on angling were written, but in the seventeenth century the diverse philosophies and methods proposed by Izaak Walton, Thomas Barker, Robert Venables, Charles Cotton, and others catalyzed a more thorough definition of sport-fishing.

Although Walton himself eventually came to be revered as the patron saint of fly-fishing, his main contribution to angling was more literary than practical in contrast to that made by his protégé Cotton.

Cotton's input to fly-fishing was that of a truly knowledgeable angling writer. He was more or less the Joe Brooks of his time and would probably have ranked at the top of the list of most popular modern fishing writers had his birthday occurred a few centuries later. For Cotton was *the* fly-fishing pioneer of his times, the innovator who was first to define the importance of finesse and fine tackle for trout fishing. And it was during his time that tackle technology began an era of development and innovation.

Exactly when a fishing rod using a free-running, loose line came into use isn't clear, but there is evidence from Barker's writings that it was at least 300 years ago. The fishing reel probably had its beginnings about the same time. In his book *The Complete Troller* (1682), Robert Nobbes suggested using 30 yards of line wound on a "roll that turns upon a ring," i.e. some sort of primitive reel-like line-carrying device. Later in the same passage he made a reference also to casting; he said "it will be ready to cast out and you may throw it farther." Cotton had placed considerable importance on casting with a fly rod some six years earlier in the fifth edition of *The Compleat Angler*. And based on the known capabilities of early-day and modern fly rods, one can safely assume he was casting a tapered horsehair fly line up to 40 feet, possibly more.

Other anglers of Cotton's era to refer in their writings to casting equipment and techniques included John Dennys, who in a poem entitled *The Secrets of Angling* made the first known reference to a rod built of whole cane.

One of the earliest references to a reel appeared in Thomas Barker's *Barker's Delight*. He called the primitive device a "winder."

Fishing rods of the seventeenth century would be considered very primitive by modern standards. Most were long, heavy, and cumbersome. The earliest wood casting rods were made in as many as six joints, or sections. Their butt sections were usually crafted from strong, springy woods like hickory or ash. Close-grained woods like greenheart and lancewood were preferred for tip joints because of their elasticity and toughness. Whalebone was also used for tips on some of the early casting rods.

The casting instruments of the seventeenth century may have had their shortcomings, but they hooked a lot of fish for the better part of a century before additional improvements took place in rod-building technique and choice of materials. Experimentation most certainly occurred during that time, but little came of it until the nineteenth century. It was a different story when it came to fishing reels.

The Multiplying Reel

By 1734 at least one sort of relatively sophisticated reel was being manufactured in England. And by 1760 the London reel-maker Onesimus Ustonson was marketing multiplying brass reels. Ustonson's reels were the forerunners of present-day multiplying, level-wind bait-casting reels.

Examples of English multiplying reels eventually reached North America and found their way to Kentucky, where they underwent "Americanization." The first really important improvements over the British multipliers were made by George Snyder, who was president of the Bourbon Angling Club in 1810. During the following decades, several other master watchmakers turned their inventiveness to improving upon the Snyder reel, including Jonathan Fleming Meek, his brother B. F. Meek, J. W. Hardman, and William Shakespeare, Jr.

Hardman's reel, on which the spool diameter was widened and its length shortened, was the first major improvement over Snyder's famous Kentucky reel.

Shakespeare began making fishing reels in Kalamazoo, Michigan, about the turn of the century. He perfected the level-winding reel about 1900. Before his important innovation, anglers had to distribute the line back and forth on the spool with their fingers. The level-winding device accomplished this automatically, making possible more efficient playing of hooked fish.

About the same time Shakespeare was perfecting the level-wind reel, the Enterprise Manufacturing Company of Akron, Ohio, was formed by the immigrant mold and pattern maker E. F. Pfleuger. The Pfleuger Supreme bait-casting reel

Fig. 1. Spinning brought casting out of the "dark ages."

his firm brought out before the First World War—now incorporating some notable improvements, of course—remains extremely popular to this day.

The Spinning Reel

Spinning reels as we know them today underwent a similar period of development.

In 1840, an Englishman by the name of Samuel Lowkes designed the Nottingham reel, which featured a delicately balanced, pivoted drum. During that same era, a free-running reel, the Scarborough, came into use by British coastal anglers. The design relied on finger pressure on the reel drum for braking power, and a form of it is still used by British anglers to this day. With it a skilled caster is said to be able to make casts in excess of 200 feet with 35-pound-test braided line.

Another important forerunner of the spinning reel came on the scene in 1884 when P. D. Mal-loch of Perth, England, patented the Malloch casting reel. Line payed off freely from the drum over the spool flange, effectively eliminating the momentum problems generated by drum rotation in reels of the center-pin design. But it was necessary to rotate the drum in order to recover line with Malloch's reel, which in turn put a bothersome twist in the line.

The line-twist problem was effectively solved in the early twentieth century when Alfred Holden Illingworth of England adapted the principles of the loom spindle to fishing reels. His Illingworth No. 1, patented in 1905, was the first truly fixed-spool spinning reel. Ultimately, the design spawned a host of more advanced spinning reels both in England and Europe, and later after World War II in America.

Illingworth's reel solved the line-twist problem peculiar to reels of the Malloch type. Its 3:1 recovery ratio made possible for the first time some really effective upstream bait and lure fishing in fast-flowing waters. It also eliminated the need for excessively long casting rods, although that isn't to say that the tradition-steeped British caster was willing to accept this fact right off the bat. Subsequent refinements, like the slipping clutch, made possible fishing with very fine-diameter light-test lines—a sport that was referred to in England as thread-line fishing and in North America later as ultra-light spinning.

Following the end of the Second World War, some of the first European and British reels to find their ways to this country in the war bags of returning GI's were the French-made Luxor, the Swiss Fix, and the British-made Hardex, Altex, and Ambidex reels. Some were offered with either manual or mechanical line-pickup devices.

In case you haven't seen one of the manual-pickup reels, the line literally must be picked up at the completion of the cast with the index finger of the casting hand, then placed on a roller guide before commencing the retrieve.

Early mechanical line pickups were usually in the form of metal fingers which were snapped into an open position before the cast was made, rather in the way the modern bail is opened, then clicked back into the winding position with a turn of the reel handle.

One of the first American-made spinning reels to appear after the war was the Bache-Brown Airex Mastereel, which was manufactured by the Lionel Corporation in New York. It was practically identical to the Luxor reel in design and operation.

The Ambidex was one of the classiest of the postwar-era spinning reels to achieve a degree of popularity on this side of the big pond. It was manufactured by the respected firm of J. W. Young & Co., Ltd., and readily converted from right- to left-handed operation.

Possibly the most popular foreign-made spinning reel ever to reach North America is the French-made Mitchell reel, which was introduced about 25 years ago. According to Richard C. Wolff, vice president of the Garcia Corporation, which distributes the reel in the U.S., a fellow named Jacquemin designed the gear mechanism that made this high-performance reel possible. Essentially, the Mitchell reel eliminates the pause as the spool changes direction. The mechanism features a double rack actuated by three fingers located on the transfer gear. Thus, when the spool is fully retracting, the first finger of the transfer gear is immediately ready to shove forward again, preventing line pile-up at the ends of the spool.

The Spin-Casting Reel

Spin-cast reels are products of the postwar era and are truly all-American designs. During that period, open-faced spinning reels were just starting to achieve some popularity here. But bait-casting with revolving-spool multiplying reels was also in its popular heyday. Quite a large number of casters favoring multiplying reels with level-winds found the longer, relatively limber spinning rods almost as objectionable as cranking the new-fangled "coffee grinder" reels, as they called the open-faced spinning reels.

To be sure, more open-minded anglers could usually see and appreciate the definite advantages of the fixed-spool design. So it wasn't illogical that eventually someone would adapt the fixed-spool design to a reel that would suit the short, stiff American bait-casting rods with offset handles.

The first spin-cast reel was the Ashaway Slip-cast reel, which allowed inexperienced casters to toss out lures and baits without annoying backlashes. But along with some of the other early spin-cast reels, it eventually faded from the scene.

One of the first practical spin-cast reels was the Zebco Model 12, first marketed in 1949. But it had a drawback, like some other early reels of its type: It couldn't accommodate casting very lightweight baits and lures.

Lloyd E. Johnson and H. Warren Denison founded Johnson Reels at Mankato, Minnesota. In 1955, that firm brought out its first Model 100 Century reel, which represented a departure from what are known as the old "sidewinder" reels, an early type in which the monofilament line was delivered out of the reel's side instead of a nose-cone at the front end.

The Model 100 was so successful that its basic design is the basis of many popular spin-cast reels to this day. Its development led to a whole new range of ideas, and today Johnson Reels holds sixteen U.S. patents as well as Canadian and Japanese patents. Many U.S. and foreign manufacturers are licensed to use these patents.

Finally, in 1953, Zebco came out with what is considered by some to be the best of the early spin-cast reels, their Model 33. It would cast lightweight lures and incorporated a slipping clutch. Now incorporating improvements that have been made down through the years, the Zebco Model 33 remains a popular favorite.

By the mid-1950s, the Garcia Corporation had achieved distinction in the tackle-marketing busi-

Fig. 2.   A present-day spin-casting reel.

ness as a result of introducing the Mitchell spinning reel to American anglers. In 1957 they began to import the Abu 60, a Swedish-made spin-casting reel of superb quality and performance. Following that model's success, they introduced the Abu 40, and later the Abu 70, a reel intended for use with lines up to 15-pound-test, ideal for the bass angler who wanted to use spin-casting equipment for fishing plastic worms and spinner baits.

Today, most major reel manufacturers in America are producing and marketing spin-cast reels of excellent quality, including Shakespeare, Pfleuger, Horrocks-Ibbotson, Langley, and Wright & McGill.

The Split-Cane Era

One of the truly important developments in the history of fishing-tackle design took place in the nineteenth century with popularization of the solid, split-cane method of casting-rod construction. In a sense, it's rather surprising that the method of splitting, fitting, and gluing together sections of bamboo cane into solid rods didn't receive more attention in the western world much earlier. The Chinese had written about it as early as the third century B.C.

But when the method was rediscovered, it created an almost immediate flurry of experimentation and controversy.

Samuel Phillippe, an Easton, Pennsylvania, gunmaker, has been credited with being the inventor of the split-bamboo fishing rod in 1862. However, a New York *Times* article in 1881 credits E. A. Green of Newark, New Jersey, as

"having made a fine bamboo rod for his own use" in 1860. The same article pointed out that Charles F. Murphy "turned out the first split-bamboo rod for trout fishing in 1863."

Not that it makes a great deal of difference, but it could well be that the real credit for the accomplishment belongs to an English rod-maker. Edward Fitzgibbon wrote about using three-strip split-cane tip and second joints on his personal salmon rods in 1847.

Whoever it was that really invented the split-cane rod—ancient Chinese craftsman, American or English rod-builder of the nineteenth century—anglers throughout the world owe him a debt of gratitude. The rods of split bamboo were infinitely superior to the long, cumbersome rods of solid hardwoods.

Not only did the new structural material allow craftsmen to control a rod's stiffness to a greater degree, thereby permitting them to conceive more effective rod actions, but it also allowed significant reduction in rod length and weight. The end result was lighter, shorter, quicker, more powerful rods than had previously been considered possible.

Theoretically, at least, a fishing rod built of split cane is most efficient when made from three splines (sections) of the cane material. But what looked good to early craftsmen in theory didn't prove out in practice. The natural curve of the cane presented some troublesome problems during the gluing process.

Rod-builder Charles Murphy was one of the first to recognize that split cane's future lay in rods of more than three splines. He began to experiment with six-strip construction as early as 1864. His first rods were of quadrate (four-strip) design, a style that didn't really become popular until much later.

By 1870, construction of bamboo fishing rods had become a highly competitive activity in the United States. And it was Hiram Leonard of Bangor, Maine, who probably did the most to project the six-strip split-cane fishing rod into the popular role it played until after World War II.

Leonard introduced Tonkin cane (also known as tea-stick bamboo) to the rod-building trade, although his early rods were of lancewood and ash. The first Leonard rod was built about 1871. It was four-sided. But Leonard's engineering knowledge forced him to conclude that rods with six splines had some distinct advantages over those made with fewer strips of the tough, resilient Asian grass.

Leonard started his rod-making enterprise at

the time when the Civil War was drawing to a close, and as a result of his superb craftsmanship and that of skilled assistants at his Bangor shop, the business flourished. Eventually, the names of Payne, Edwards, and Thomas, all Bangor craftsmen trained by Leonard, became famous in their own right.

Leonard eventually went into partnership with William Mills and Son of New York City and moved the factory to Central Valley in Orange County, New York.

Thomas, Edwards, and Payne left Leonard's firm about the turn of the century and ultimately set up their own rod-making companies. It wasn't long before they each developed circles of staunchly loyal customers. Edwards later popularized an incredibly fine fly rod of quadrate design.

Charles F. Orvis, of Manchester, Vermont, started making fishing rods in 1856. Like Leonard, his early rods were made of lancewood, but he soon became persuaded of the superiority of split cane and transferred his attention to it.

An innovator of the first order, he obtained a patent on his first fly reel on May 12, 1874. It was a new concept in American-made reels with its narrow spool and perforated side plates.

Orvis' petition for letters of patent stated that the reel had perforated side plates of hard rubber, to allow the line to dry, and added that the side plates could also be made of metal.

According to Austin Hogan, hard rubber was never used in the commercial models. The first were made out of a white metal. Modifications made in the immediate years following included removal of an outside protective side plate, addition of a balance weight, and elimination of the handle bar. Later, the reel was enlarged and the handles were changed to create the first Orvis Bass Reel.

Orvis also produced, in 1882, the first spring-lock reel seat made for an American-made rod, and he was the first American rod-builder to use cork grips on fly-rod handles.

Wes Jordan, acknowledged dean of present-day split-cane craftsmen, joined Orvis in 1940. Before that he had been employed by the Cross Rod Company, which eventually merged with the South Bend Company. While at Cross, Jordan developed several machines for constructing accurate production split-cane rods. In 1942, he joined with McClure of the Smithsonian Institution in a study of bamboo species of the western hemisphere. His contributions to the art and craft of building fine casting instruments also include

introduction of Orvis' beautiful walnut reel seats, development of a new type of locking reel seat, designing equipment for building quality cane rods by mass-production methods, and perfecting the impregnation process which distinguishes present-day Orvis rods.

The Bakelite impregnation process has been refined over the years from its original form as conceived by engineer Everett Garrison of Ossining, New York, but essentially what takes place is that the resin waterproofs the bamboo so completely that varnishing the rod's outer surface is unnecessary. The resin also tends to bind the splines into a stick of incredible resistance to moisture.

Charles Orvis himself is also credited with marketing the first commercially made fly reels in the United States and being the first to get a patent on the click-reel.

By the mid-1930s, a number of other craftsmen both on and beyond the eastern seaboard were producing quite a wide selection of fine split-cane casting instruments. They included Granger, Phillipson, Powell, Dickerson, Heddon, Young, Cross, and Stoner. Five-sided rods were also being popularized at that time by Bishop of Hillburn, New York, Uslan of Spring Valley, New York, Frank Wire of Portland, Oregon, and Paul Young.

Hardy Bros. of England has been the most famous name in the U.S. associated with high-quality split-cane casting rods of foreign manufacture. They are still made today and marketed here by Harrington & Richardson. Cortland Line Company presently markets under its name a line of very good split-bamboo fly rods produced in England. Pezon et Michel of France also sells significant numbers of excellent cane rods in the United States.

Rod Actions—
Organized Confusion

During split cane's heyday, rod actions were described by their makers as being either dry-fly, wet-fly, bass-bug, or steelhead/salmon. This tended to be confusing to the generally unsophisticated American angling public, and there was sometimes quite a broad difference of opinion in defining those terms on the part of rod craftsmen themselves.

Today, manufacturers are a bit more in semantic tune with one another. Most refer to their rods as either slow, medium, or fast in action, or as to

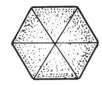

Fig. 3. Split-cane cross-sections for four-, five-, and six-sided rods.

whether they're designed for light-, medium-, or heavy-duty casting.

One of the more interesting and better-casting rod actions to be popularized in the 1930s was the so-called parabolic rod. The name was catchy and fresh, although a bit of a misnomer, but the action itself was an old one hailing back well into the 1800s. What it described was a full-flexing rod with a kind of double action.

Genio C. Scott, author of *Fishing in American Waters,* in 1875 referred to rods with both single and double actions. He described a double-action rod as one with a kick in the handle and pointed out that a single-action rod had more snap when striking a fish, but that a double-action one would cast a line farther and would deliver a fly more delicately.

That distinction rather closely describes the parabolic rods that came on the scene in the next century. And although most knowledgeable casters are now aware of the error in nomenclature, they still refer to such casting instruments with deep affection, using the word that really describes a plane curve formed by the intersection of a cone by a plane parallel to the side of the cone—a shape, not a feel.

Once the word "parabolic" came on the scene in reference to rod action, additional confusion resulted with the development of the "semi-parabolic action," which was slightly more flexible in the tip than the fully parabolic stick; and the "semi-parabolic action with supple tip"—also known as the "compound taper." It boasted a butt taper, a relatively untapered middle section, and a tapered tip joint. The "progressive taper," which describes a rod in which the taper extends the entire length of the rod, and the "tournament action," which had feel down through the butt but a taper unlike the parabolic, were also spawned during the same era.

American rod-building technology made tremendous progress in the split-cane era, but it took from Leonard's time until the 1940s for fly-fishing to really catch on as a widely accepted sport throughout North America.

Casting's Golden Age

Virtually all of the premier-grade rods made during the 1862–1945 period were solid-polygon construction, as shown in Fig. 3. The splines of the best were hand-split, planed to matching tolerances of approximately .001 inch, then glued and wrapped together under pressure. But even with the coming of Tonkin cane (*Arundinaria amabilis*), it was evident to certain of the rod-builders that solid rods were not the final product to be achieved from the superbly resilient grass, the only known habitat of which was a 25-mile-long area near the boundary between Kwangsi and Kwangtung provinces northwest of Canton in southern China. (Tonkin cane does *not* come from Tonkin province of North Vietnam.)

Innovators on both sides of the Atlantic continued to experiment with split cane. Hardy Bros. of England and the Cross Rod Company in the U.S. both made double-built (rod inside of rod) rods for a time. Hardy Bros. produced some with steel cores for heavy-duty fly-casting and spinning.

Another imaginative American craftsman, Lou Stoner, was intrigued with the possibilities of an engineering form, the arched beam. But briefly preceding his significant efforts, an important event took place in fly-line design.

Until 1934 or thereabouts, all American-made fly lines had been of either level or double-tapered construction. Then came the torpedo-head line, in which the casting weight was concentrated dramatically toward one end, thus increasing the caster's ability to make long casts.

It was Lou Stoner, one of the trade's true master craftsmen, who brought out a fly rod to utilize the line's full potential. He developed and patented a fly rod in which the butt section was hollow-fluted with a series of minute arched beams. The result was a tournament fly rod of incredible stiffness and lightness, fast recovery speed, and strength, and within the 5¾-ounce rod-weight restriction of the trout-fly tourney games of the times. That was in 1938. And the effect of mating Stoner's rod with the torpedo-head line was no less than record-shattering.

The first hollow-butt rods built by Stoner's firm, R. L. Winston Rods, were so powerful that few casters outside the tournament circuit could fully master their potential. But Marvin Hedge of Portland, Oregon, was one who could. That same year he set a new world record, topping the previous one by over 36 feet. The following year, Dick Miller set still another record with a phenomenal cast of 183 feet 3 inches.

Stoner passed away in 1957, but he left his legacy of skillful artistry in rod design and construction to Doug Merrick, who continues to maintain the Stoner tradition to this day in San Francisco.

Steel Rods

The end of World War I kicked off an era of mass production in tackle manufacturing in America. During the early 1920s, the True Temper Corporation brought out the first solid-steel fishing rods. Anglers were somewhat slow to accept them at the time, but they gradually gained popularity because of their virtual indestructibility and low price.

Heddon, which had achieved great renown as a manufacturer of fine split-cane fly and bait-casting rods, brought out their first steel rod in 1930. The tips were purchased from True Temper and fitted with Heddon's detachable butts and locking reel seats. In 1933, they brought out their own steel rod—a tubular model that was advertised as "The Rod of Steel with Bamboo Feel." And that same year, Heddon patented a greatly improved bait-casting rod handle, which had an offset, a screw-locking reel seat, a sliding hood, and a screw-locking tip.

During the decade before the start of World War II, the U.S. angling market was dominated primarily by split-cane and steel casting instruments.

The Fiberglass Era

Split cane was finally challenged for its position as the premier rod-building material immediately following World War II. When the gauntlet was thrown, the contest was fatal—to split cane.

According to Browning Arms Co., the first fiberglass rod was made in 1944 by Jim Lawhead at the National Research and Manufacturing Co. in National City, California. It was a hexagon-shaped solid-glass rod made in a matched metal die from woven glass cloth. Three or four experimental rods were made.

The Shakespeare Company, however, probably deserves most of the credit for starting bamboo's demise. The cutting off of trade with China in the 1950s cost us our source of the traditional raw cane culms and, of course, took split cane out of competition.

During World War II, Dr. Arthur M. Howald,

then technical director of the Plaskon Division of Libbey-Owens-Ford Glass Company, experimented with a heat-hardened resin. When reinforced with fine fiberglass fibers, it was used to make certain aircraft parts.

Howald perceived similarities between the glass-plastic combination and the qualities provided by nature in natural bamboo cane. He experimented with fly rods made from the glass-resin product. The results of his work were turned over to the Shakespeare Company and several experimental rods were field-tested under difficult conditions.

Laboratory tests were conducted to determine the strength, ability to withstand set, water resistance, and other characteristics of the new rods. After testing proved the product's mettle, sample models were established and machinery designed to actually produce rods. Bait-casting rods were produced first. Fly rods followed later.

A million dollars went into the first Shakespeare fiberglass Wonderod, which reached anglers in 1946. In a sense, its development was the beginning of a revolution in fishing-rod manufacturing which continues to this day. For the first time in history, a successful attempt had been made to duplicate to varying degrees by synthetic means the qualities found in natural Tonkin cane. And although hundreds of different brands of fiberglass rods are now produced, Shakespeare alone enjoys exclusive use of Howald's fabricating process.

It was logical at the time to assume additional processes using other forms of fiberglass-resin matrix materials would soon follow. And they did, some almost simultaneously. Some of the early rods were made in solid construction in both round and polygon shapes. Others used either woven fiberglass fabrics or unidirectional fibers formed on precisely ground steel mandrels to form hollow, tubular shapes.

The idea for forming glass-resin material around a mandrel probably resulted from the wartime need for a new fly rod by Robert L. Pigg, a photo-chemist with Consolidated Vultee Aircraft Corporation. Bob Pigg was an accomplished flycaster who had been taught the craft of rodmaking by his father, Ben.

One day, Bob spotted a radio antenna on a police car and wondered if it would serve to ding up some kind of rod. He tried an antenna rod and converted it for saltwater fishing. But he wasn't quite satisfied with the antenna fishing rod and built a rod from a glass fiber-plastic mixture. This second attempt proved to be acceptable for bait-casting, but too large in diameter for fly-casting.

The next step came when Bob Pigg took a steel antenna and tried to use it as a mandrel. But the core diameter was too large, so he had some special steel mandrels made up.

After more than a year of painstaking experimentation, during which a lot of technical problems had to be overcome, Bob Pigg constructed the first tubular glass freshwater fly rod. Pigg ordered his first mandrel from the Coast Centerless Grinding Company of Los Angeles, California. In 1946, with his father and brother-in-law, he formed the California Tackle Company and contracted with a local firm that made hollow fiberglass tubing to produce hollow glass fishing-rod blanks to specifications supplied by and on mandrels owned by California Tackle. The first rods made by the company were sold in early 1947 to the Western Tackle Company of Los Angeles.

Conolon, under the name of National Research and Manufacturing Company, produced and sold the very first unidirectional glass tubular rods formed on steel mandrels in 1945, according to Conolon Corporation president Howard A. Ashby, though prototypes were probably made as early as 1943 under the direction of Dr. Glenn Havens, then research and development director of Convair, and later principal owner of Narmco, which was the derivative of the National Research and Manufacturing Company.

One of the interesting sidelights to come out of the author's research for this chapter is that all of the early tubular fiberglass rods can be traced directly to the original Narmco glass rods.

Pacific Laminates was formed as a partnership by five ex-Narmco employees in 1948, according to T. David Zeigler of Browning. They produced rod blanks under the name Sila-Flex. That firm was sold to Ekco Products of Chicago, Illinois, in 1960 and was purchased by the Browning Arms Co. two years later.

The Harrington Reynolds Company was producing casting-rod handles and selling them to Narmco, according to Zeigler. After being in the Narmco plant and seeing what was done, he says they set up and produced the Harnel rod. Ben Pigg was, of course, an early customer of Narmco and Sila-Flex. He later set up and manufactured his own fishing-rod blanks.

The first mandrels for tubular glass rods were made on a lathe at great expense. When additional mandrels were needed, the project was turned over to Harold Hogarth. He was so intrigued with the potential that he quit his job and bought a centerless grinder to produce them. He started in his garage, and since he couldn't get a permit for electric power in his garage, he bought a Model A engine and ran his grinding machine with his wife at the throttle to control the speed. Today, Hogarth and his company, the Linco Grinding Company of Los Angeles, produce mandrels for virtually all of the world's glass-rod makers.

The Garcia/Conolon Corporation, formerly the Conolon Corporation, was formed in 1961, when the Garcia Corporation acquired Conolon. Before then, Garcia was the sole distributor of Conolon rods under the Garcia name, starting in 1949.

When Michael M. Stocker acquired controlling interest in the California Tackle Company in the 1960s, he decided to develop what he hoped would be the finest fiberglass fishing rod on the market. Stocker experimented and continues to test virtually every possible type of potential rod-building material in his search for the better fishing rod. He was responsible for developing his own special process utilizing shrink cellophane wrappings on the glass-resin matrix material after it was wrapped on the mandrel. He says the shrink cellophane, unlike other types in use, puts tremendous pressure on the materials and alleviates many of the porosity problems encountered with other methods of fiberglass-rod construction.

Today, Stocker's firm produces custom-built fiberglass tubular rods and rod blanks of the highest quality under the tradename Sabre. According to Stocker, his is the only company of its kind to provide a custom rod design and manufacturing service to tackle shops and to custom glass-rod builders like Harry D. Wilson, custom craftsman producing the Scott rods, and Yo Yoshida, builder of custom saltwater rods in Gardena, California.

In 1958, the Sevenstrand Tackle Manufacturing Company acquired the Jim Green Line Company and along with it the services of the multi-talented Green himself. Jim Green is one of the really great tournament casters who appeared in the years following World War II. In 1959, Sevenstrand acquired the Fenwick Rod Company, which had operated in Washington State since 1953. And in January 1962, Fenwick/Sevenstrand brought out their first Feralite fishing rods, excellent casting instruments without ferrules, the design parameters of which Green had worked on for several years. The unique ferruleless design swept the fishing marketplace by storm, practically eliminating the ferrule from multi-section tubular glass rods for the first time. Today, many rod-manufacturing firms have developed ferruleless designs of their own, and the glass-to-glass mating of rod joints is generally preferred by those anglers who desire continuity of action without "dead spots."

But that was just the beginning for Fenwick. About five years before this writing, it became apparent to them that while they could achieve very desirable and efficient actions using fiberglass, the ultimate materials remained to be discovered and developed. Jim Green, working in conjunction with Don Green (who is no relation to Jim) at Fenwick's Washington State blank factory, began to experiment with what are now referred to as "advanced materials." These included du Pont PDR materials, boron, and carbon-graphite fibers.

Their studies resulted in the discovery that carbon-graphite fibers are easily worked into fabrics which can be used in tubular rod construction in much the same way as fiberglass. Carbon fibers are not only readily obtainable (at a vastly higher cost to the manufacturer than fiberglass, I might add) but are also available in a range of property combinations.

Other great names from the ranks of tournament casting entered the rod-design field about the same time. The late world all-round casting champion, Jon Tarantino of San Francisco, teamed with Hardy Bros. to design a U.S.-made fiberglass fly rod of excellent quality that was ultimately marketed under the Hardy name.

In 1968, Scientific Anglers, Inc., of Midland, Michigan, one of the pioneer developers of modern plastic-coated American-made fly lines, teamed with Hardy Bros. and Jon Tarantino to create the "System" rods and reels, a totally new marketing concept in fly-fishing tackle.

"System" rods and reels came about as a result of Scientific Anglers president Leon Martuch noting that whenever he went fishing, he usually selected one of three or four pet rods from his sizable collection. Leon asked himself why he regularly chose the rods he did.

His conclusion was that each of the rods in question *balanced* almost perfectly with some specific weight of fly line and was particularly well suited to a certain type of fishing.

Up to that time, most anglers started with the fishing rod, then attempted to match a line to it. Martuch reversed the process. He started with lines ranging in weight from 4- to 11-weight, which covered the full range of fly-fishing situations, from ultra-light trouting to the most

Fig. 4.   Jim Green.

Fig. 5.   The late Jon Tarantino.

demanding heavy-duty saltwater fishing. Jon Tarantino designed several prototype rods for each line weight. Martuch made the final judgments about what basic action the final production model would be, taken from the prototypes for each line weight. Hardy Bros. manufactured a special high-quality single-action fly reel to match the line weight and rod size for each of the eight System rods. The reel features a wraparound spool flange

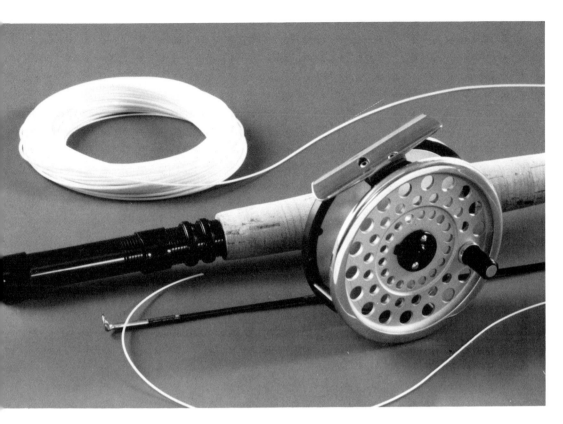

Fig. 6. The "system" concept.

which allows positive finger-braking once a heavy fish is hooked.

Martuch, who now serves as a consultant to the 3M Company, says, "We think they're the best production rods ever made. In each case, we selected a rod that would do the best job of throwing a given weight of line for the average caster."

Bill Phillipson is another of the innovators whose creativity thrust fiberglass into its own era. Phillipson was Granger's master craftsman in bamboo until that firm was sold to the Wright and McGill Co. He later formed his own firm in Denver, Colorado, and produced a remarkably fine line of bamboo casting instruments while that material still retained broad popularity and availability.

When he entered into producing fiberglass rods, the material he finally settled on was 3M's Scotchply, epoxy-impregnated continuous glass filaments in parallel alignment. Scotchply is a very strong laminate with properties that make it extremely efficient for spring use. The material is stronger than regular woven fiberglass, therefore can be loaded more. This permits making a com-

promise in design by taking out some weight from the rod. By taking cloth out, Phillipson lessened the stiffness. This resulted in the entire rod flexing, which really meant he was able to get some of the power back. His rod, from a structural standpoint, was equivalent to rods made with more material and from a casting standpoint more powerful. Phillipson Rod Company was eventually acquired by the 3M Company, which continues to manufacture the Scotchply designs of the master craftsman with great attention to maintaining the qualities he built into them.

Sila-Flex was another leader in fiberglass rod development. In 1950, they reinforced the butt actions of their rods by means of an extra fiberglass lay-up in the butt, eliminating the loose, buggywhip actions found in some early glass rods. The same firm introduced in 1953 their now famous Medallion rod series, which featured thin-wall construction resulting in a very light, lively rod that helped start the conversion of fly-casters from split cane.

In 1960, Sila-Flex began to use extreme pressures to cure fiberglass rod blanks. Their high-density pressure construction is said to produce a

Fig. 7. Phil Clock.

stronger bond between glass and resins, thoroughly chasing and compacting the resins around each strand of glass. This results in no weakening air bubbles, voids, or other invisible flaws. Sila-Flex was purchased by the Browning Arms Co. in 1962. In 1969, they introduced their own version of the glass ferrule. A special glass weave is used which has great hoop strength. Perhaps the most notable feature of the ferrule is that it's machined, the inside diameter taper reamed to the precise outside diameter of the mating butt section which lessens the chances of splitting, enlarging, or casting off the rod's tip.

Sila-Flex introduced to glass-rod building two advanced rod tapers, the progressive taper and the Magnum (R) taper.

The progressive taper is really nothing new to fishing-rod design, but it appears to have been an innovation in fiberglass-rod design in 1958, when it first came on the market. By a precise and progressive tapering off of both rod diameter and wall thickness, a smooth, powerful rod is made with no stress points. Diameter and wall thickness both decrease as the rod progresses from butt to tip. The progressive taper is versatile in that it lets one cast small lures as well as large, heavy ones, and to play down light or heavy fish with equal effectiveness.

The Magnum (R) I taper of Browning/Sila-Flex is a cross between the conventional straight taper (essentially a parabolic fly-rod action) and their progressive taper. The resulting rod is claimed to be a subtle blend of the Magnum taper's power and the straight taper's accuracy. It is used on all

present-day Browning freshwater casting, spinning, river, and surf rods.

Early in the 1960s, Phil Clock, president of Fenwick, and Jim Green conducted some static tests on the comparative fly-rod stiffness between metal, fiberglass, and split cane. Their studies determined that the stiffness profiles of two rods of comparable material give parallel casting qualities. Fenwick concluded that the carbon-graphite materials being experimented with by Green and his associates could be used to create a superior fishing rod, once the cost of the material became low enough so that rods made of it could be produced at reasonable prices.

Enter the Space-Age Fibers

With the advent of the carbon-graphite golf shaft, the price of high-modulus graphite material began to drop significantly and reached a level where fishing-rod manufacture was realistic.

The advantages of the carbon-graphite material are several. In high-temperature furnaces all components of the raw fiber are driven out except for carbon, leaving strands as small as .0003 inch in diameter. The fiber strands are then made into a yarnlike substance and impregnated with resin, which makes a workable, fabriclike, fiber-resin material. The resulting rod is much lighter than its bamboo, glass, or steel equivalents, and also smaller in diameter. As a result, more casting power can be built into a rod of very light weight and small diameter.

In 1973, Fenwick introduced their first carbon-graphite rods at the American Fishing Tackle Manufacturers Association Show in Chicago, Illinois. Prototypes of the rods were also displayed and demonstrated at the Federation of Fly Fishermen Conclave at Sun Valley, Idaho, that same summer.

The resulting production-model Fenwick HMG Graphite Rods were offered to anglers early in 1974. They're about 25 percent lighter than the lightest equivalent fiberglass rods, and some 40 percent lighter than equivalent bamboos. Chapter 4 contains more background concerning all the presently employed rod-building materials, including graphite.

Shakespeare Fly Wonderods are now also being marketed in carbon-graphite versions under the trade name Graflite Wonderods. Certainly, the innovative surge in rod-making technology is presently at its highest apogee. And perhaps the best is yet to come.

Early Fishing Lines

During Dame Juliana de Berners' times, fishing lines were braided mostly from several strands of horsehair. Horsehair lines in fairly sophisticated versions remained in use well into the nineteenth century. Joe Brooks relates in his book *Trout Fishing* having encountered them in use in a remote section of Wales even more recently.

Lines made from natural silk and linen fibers started appearing in the mid-1800s. During the transitional period, some lines made from mixtures of those fibers and horsehair also came briefly on the scene.

Silk casting lines had the market cornered by 1880. The earliest were of two types, one type made of boiled silk, the other of raw silk fibers.

Raw silk fibers unwound from the cocoon contain a gumlike substance which holds the cocoon together. Boiling removes the gummy substance and reduces the weight of the fibers by nearly a third.

The first silk fly lines were just about as flexible as modern braided bait-casting lines. Earlier writers have noted observing nineteenth-century anglers muttering traditional epithets to themselves as they tried to untangle lines knotted around their fly-rod tips. Solving the limp fly-line problem required stiffening the line somewhat. One of the first methods of accomplishing that end consisted of applying grease to the line. The next improvement was oil impregnation.

In this process, a tapered silk core is impregnated with linseed oil, then hung to dry in a tall tower. The oil polymerizes to form a solid, supple finish that is a joy to cast. However, oil-impregnated silk fly lines require lots of care.

The specific gravity of silk is greater than that of water. Therefore, when silk line is to be used for fishing dry flies, it must be first coated with something to make it float—"dressed" as anglers refer to the procedure. Once the line dressing rubs off, the line must be uncoiled from the reel and thoroughly dried out. Then a fresh coat of line dressing is applied, allowed to set for a while, and finally polished with a dry cloth. At the end of the day's fishing, the line must be removed once again from the reel (to prevent mildewing), dried, and redressed. If one of the oil-finish lines is stored unused for an extended time, the finish may soften and become gummy.

Despite all their drawbacks, oil-impregnated fly lines cast beautifully and remained the popular favorites until the development of the present-day plastic-coated ones.

To be sure, by 1885, U.S. line-makers were producing less expensive enameled silk fly lines, which had some appeal to the mass market, but were never really accepted by critical casters and fishermen. These were quickly forced off the market when the plastic-coated lines came on the scene.

Synthetic Fiber Fly Lines

Scientific Anglers, Inc., of Midland, Michigan; Cortland Line Company of Cortland, N.Y.; Ashaway Line & Twine Mfg. Co. of Ashaway, Rhode Island; and B. F. Gladding & Co. of South Otselic, New York, were probably the four firms most responsible for popularizing the use of synthetic fibers and plastic finishes in the manufacture of U.S.-made fly lines.

The first big technological breakthrough came in 1953 when Cortland introduced their 333 non-sinkable fly lines with nonporous synthetic coatings. Other major American line-makers quickly followed suit. Some of the early plastic-coated fly lines, however, had a polyvinyl-chloride coating applied as a lacquer instead of as a solvent. This finish tended to crack after extended use. In turn, water would wick into the line core, which was hollow-braided, causing the line to sink instead of float. In today's floating lines, the PVC material is plasticized by a solvent and becomes an integral part of the line structure.

Leon Martuch, Sr., of Scientific Anglers, made

Fig. 8. Plastic-coated fly lines were one of this century's major breakthroughs.

a major contribution to line manufacture by designing and patenting a unique system of applying the PVC plastisol "goop," as line-makers now refer to the coating material. A rocker-die and cam which he originated resulted in his company being able to guarantee the size and weight of the line within tolerances of ±5 grains in weight and less than .0005 inch in diameter.

Several techniques are used to enhance the floating qualities of the plastic-coated lines. Scientific Anglers has a patent on the use in fly lines of preformed glass "micro-balloons," minute glass balls of tremendous compressive strength. These are added to the goop and become an integral part of the line finish.

PVC plastic has a property that allows it to be foamed. This also allows a manufacturer to build excellent floating qualities into the line finish.

Ashaway made one of the best of the early-day synthetic floating fly lines utilizing a tapered nylon core (instead of the level core used by most manufacturers today), and a vacuum impregnation process that resulted in one of the best casting lines ever made. They marketed their first sinking fly line in 1953.

Gladding introduced their plastic-coated Aqua Sink sinking fly line in the fall of 1954, and Scientific Anglers brought out their famous Wet Cel lines in September of 1955, although they had lines out before that time. Gladding's sinking line was braided around a fine lead-wire core. Most of the others are either braided from Dacron, which has a heavier specific gravity than water, or of nylon and coated with high-density PVC.

Steps in Making a Fly Line

The reader may have noticed that some fly lines have rougher surfaces than others. This is in part due to the fact that two basic types of braided core material are used. One is a rather open basketweave, which by virtue of the weave structure tends to yield a finished line with a surface lacking glassy smoothness. This braid is used primarily to make sinking lines. The slightly roughed surface actually produces a line of extremely good casting properties. A smoother, rounder, finer-woven, hollow-core line is the basis of most present-day floating lines. The braid of this core material is finer and therefore yields a finished line with a smoother surface.

Once the line manufacturer receives a shipment of braided core line in large skeins, he flame-singes the line to remove extraneous fibers,

any of which would cause a bump in the finish once the PVC coating is applied.

The singed line is cleaned in a fluid to remove excess dye and chemicals, then primed to make it easier to apply the plastisol. Once primed, the line is preheated to boil off excess primer and cleaner. At this point, the plastisol goop is applied by means of a rocker-die which is regulated by a cam. Only one coat of plastic is necessary to make either an all-floating or an all-sinking line. Sinking-tip fly lines go through a more involved process in which the floating portion is coated first and then the sinking part. In both cases, the plastic goop is heat-cured almost instantly as it goes through the machine. The lines go to a cutting room and are separated from continuous skeins, checked for faults, rolled on 30-yard-capacity plastic spools, labeled, and shipped.

Modern methods of automated line-making have made it possible, for example, for firms like Scientific Anglers/3M to produce over 200 sizes, shapes, and colors of fly lines, including American Casting Association and International Casting Federation tournament lines, and lines for other companies under private-brand labels.

Bait-Casting Lines

By 1884, Elisha J. Martin, a silk-handler and angler of Rockville, Connecticut, was braiding some silk bait-casting lines for use by himself and his angling cronies. It wasn't long before Martin found himself in the line-manufacturing business. His firm was acquired in 1919 by Horton Manufacturing Company of Bristol, Connecticut.

The popular braided-silk bait-casting lines of the early twentieth century were made in a squarish shape—four-sided around a silk core. This was so the line would lie flat on the spool and, to a degree, reduce the chances of snarls and backlashes forming during the cast. These lines cast very well until they became overly soaked in water.

Nylon casting lines quickly replaced the silk ones in popularity once manufacturers solved early problems of excessive stretch and stickiness, which was in the mid-1940s.

Modern braided nylon and Dacron casting lines go through an amazing number of processing steps, including doubling, twisting, heat-stretching, dyeing, waterproofing, and testing. Interestingly enough, the largest number of world-record catches have been made on them. And according to the Cortland Line Company, fishermen still

Fig. 9. Bait-casting still retains great popularity.

spend as much money on braided lines as they do on monofilament, the reason being that multiplying level-wind bait-casting reels retain their popularity. On these reels, the braided lines tend to lie down and behave better than mono. They also lack mono's stretch, can be made in either floating or sinking versions, and resist scuffing extremely well.

Monofilament Lines

Monofilament nylon materials came on the scene near the end of World War II, at about the same time spinning tackle was introduced to the American market. In a sense, they catalyzed each other's popularity. The qualities of monofilament will be discussed at length elsewhere in this book.

Today, monofilament fishing lines come in a tremendous range of stiffnesses—from very hard to extremely limp, as well as in both round and flattish cross-sectional shapes. They are available in sizes ranging from less than 1-pound-test to over 100-pound-test.

Fig. 10. Monofilament has revolutionized lines and leaders.

Chapter 2

Casting Tackle

Rod Types

Three basic types of casting instruments enjoy broad popularity with North American anglers. They are referred to specifically as fly rods, spinning rods, and bait-casting rods. English anglers usually lump the latter two categories into a single one—spinning rods.

Within these generic groupings, one also finds types of rods intended for specialized kinds of fishing or casting, such as midge-type fly rods designed to carry very lightweight lines, and various types of customized tournament rods for distance casting and accuracy.

Fly rods are designed to cast fly lines. They come in a considerable range of lengths, actions, and fittings adapting them to the wide variety of freshwater and marine angling conditions. Fly-fishing is adaptable to angling for most of the important gamefish species. Conditions limiting the use of the fly rod include extremely high winds and the depth at which fish lie. If the fish are at depths exceeding 30 feet, other angling methods are usually more practical.

Reels made for use on fly rods are available in three main types: single-action, multiplying single-action, and automatic. The characteristics of each type of reel will be dealt with later in this chapter.

Fly lines are made in six standard tapered shapes as well as in level, untapered form. The functions and uses of each type and shape of tapered line will be discussed a little later, but for the time being the tyro caster should know that most tapered fly lines are available in floating, intermediate, sinking-tip, and completely sinking versions, each of which has some very definite applications to fishing and casting.

Spinning rods are designed for use with open-faced spinning reels of two basic types. Mastery of the tackle takes less practice than is required to cast effectively with either bait-casting or fly rods. As a result, it is one of the two most popular angling methods used in North America today—the other being spin-casting, a simplified form of bait-casting. Spinning tackle is adaptable to angling for every major sport fish found in U.S. and Canadian fresh and marine waters, including all the trouts, basses, panfish, salmons, and big-game and bottom-inhabiting saltwater species.

Both braided and monofilament casting lines may be used effectively on open-faced spinning reels. Mono lines are far and away the most popular for freshwater angling. Prior to the late 1940s, when monofilament had been improved to where it was a practical casting line, fishermen had little choice other than braided lines and those made of Japanese gut, a twisted, hard-finished synthetic gut made from natural silk fibers hardened with a gluelike substance.

Bait-casting rods are designed to cast weights varying from under ⅜ ounce to several ounces, and to utilize either closed-faced spin-casting or level-wind multiplying bait-casting reels. Virtually all present-day single-handed bait-casting rods are equipped with offset handles. Most double-handed bait-casting rods are equipped with straight handles.

Casting with the level-wind multiplying reel is considerably more complex than casting with the closed-face spin-casting reel. However, a correctly balanced and finely adjusted reel of this type affords the angler maximum accuracy and line control. The closed-face spin-casting reel is even easier to use than the open-faced spinning reel. The design virtually eliminates any possibility of a line snarl or backlash. As a result, it's often the best reel with which to teach the beginner the rudiments of bait-casting.

Classes of Rods

Casting rods of all the basic types may be defined both in terms of their relative lengths and the qualities of work to which they're put.

Ultra-light rods are made in both spinning and fly-casting types. The fly rods in this class are normally built to handle 3-, 4-, and 5-weight lines and usually vary from 5½ to 7½ feet long. Ultra-light spinning rods are designed to cast lures or baits weighing $5/_{16}$ ounce or less and to use lines in the ¾-pound-test to 6-pound-test range.

Combination fly-spinning rods are also made in ultra-light versions. Normally built into back-packer models consisting of four or five short sections, they're a strong preference of anglers who do a lot of fishing in high mountain lakes and streams where lightness and compactness influence the choice almost as much as utility.

Ultra-light fishing tackle is mostly used in freshwater lakes and streams. But properly handled, it's capable of whipping down the largest freshwater and anadromous sport fishes, as well

Fig. 11. Big pike are ideal bait-casting game.

as saltwater species like corbina and bonito. Ultra-light fishing tackle is probably most adaptable to trout and panfish angling in conjunction with flies, tiny spinner and wobbling lures, and baits like live insects, minnows, miniature marshmallows, cheese baits, and single cured salmon eggs. Ultra-light spinning tackle is also used to fish with flies off tiny bobbers or with several small split shot clamped to the line. In some regions, it's used for fishing feathered lures, live minnows, and pork-rind strip-baits for crappies and sunfish.

Light- to medium-duty fly rods are normally associated with 6-, 7-, and 8-weight fly lines. Rods in this class are usually designed to cast efficiently to moderate distances approaching 75 feet. They are by far the most popular class of fly rods for fishing trout, smallmouth bass, and panfish waters and range in length from 6½ to 8½ feet.

Spinning and bait-casting rods for medium-duty angling span a wide range of lengths—from about 5 to 8½ feet long. They're used mainly for general-purpose stream and lake fishing, and light-duty surf-casting. Lures and baits used on this work-class of casting instrument range in weight from ⁵⁄₁₆ to ½ ounce.

Heavy-duty fly rods are made primarily either to effect long casts or whip down very heavy gamefish in salt water, fast-flowing rivers, and lakes containing an abundance of underwater obstructions. They're designed to balance with 9-, 10-, and 11-weight fly lines, 9 weight being the most popular. American-made fly rods in this class run from 8½ to 9½ feet long. They're used in fresh water for bass, pike, muskellunge, Atlantic salmon, Pacific salmon, and steelhead fishing. In salt water, heavy-duty and extra-heavy-duty fly rods are used on species ranging up to several hundred pounds in weight.

Heavy-duty spinning and bait-casting rods vary tremendously in length, stiffness, and action. The shortest are usually about 5 feet long and made expressly for horsing bass, pike, and muskies out of the snags and weeds. Longer versions vary considerably in action, and include both stiff and supple-tipped models. Lures used with rods of this class vary from roughly ⅝ ounce to several ounces in weight.

Rod Actions

When a casting rod is bent, the act of bending it is called flexing the rod. The shape a rod assumes when flexed and released influences how it feels in the hand and how it causes a fly line to behave. Its ability to be flexed affects the amount of potential energy that it can store and release into the cast line or lure. The speed at which a rod recovers from bending is called its recovery rate. And it is this latter factor that we refer to most when describing rod action. Other factors involved in the definition of action include flexibility and effective stiffness. All of these qualities, and others, will be discussed at considerable length in Chapter 4, which deals with the dynamics of casting and casting instruments.

Building Your Own Rod

Casting rods are mostly made from one of three basic materials—split bamboo cane, unidirectional or woven fiberglass, or carbon-graphite fibers. The characteristics of these materials will be discussed in Chapter 4.

At this writing, fiberglass rods are priced to fit virtually anyone's budget—from about $1.95 to nearly $300. Quality split-cane rods vary from about $80 to $250. Carbon-graphite rods sell variously from about $125 to $200.

Nevertheless, building one's own casting rods has become a popular diversion, both to save money and to obtain a true custom rod.

An angler can purchase all the components needed to assemble a first-rate fiberglass or split-cane rod at savings often exceeding 50 percent of the retail selling price of comparable-action factory- or custom-built rods. If the home craftsman is meticulous, chances are his efforts will result in rods that equal in aesthetic appeal and performance those made by custom craftsmen.

Split-cane rod assembly kits usually sell for a bit over $85 (for a fly rod), including the ferruled sections, a preformed cork-ring grip, a high-quality reel seat, guides, tip-top, keeper ring, rod-wrapping thread, color preserver, and finishing material.

Complete fiberglass rod kits contain the same essential components and range in price from under $20 to over $50. Even better prices can be realized by those who take the trouble to locate outlets where components may be obtained at the lowest possible prices.

Although quite a few books contain brief sections on fiberglass-rod assembling techniques, it should be noted that there's now a very good book devoted to the subject, *Fiberglass Rod Making* by Dale P. Clemens (Winchester Press, 1974).

Fig. 12. A home-built fiberglass rod landed this dandy trout.

In some cases, it's also possible for the enthusi-
ast to learn the rather complex art of building
split-cane rods from the raw culm up. Classes are
conducted by a few U.S. clubs. However, split-
cane-rod building requires a great deal of time,
patience, and the highest possible quality of
instruction—and the last is available in only a few
locations.

Fly Lines

Virtually all American fly-line manufacturers use
line cores braided from either nylon or Dacron
fibers. Synthetic fly lines are superior to the old-
time silks for a number of reasons. The silk lines,
being made from natural fibers, were inconsistent
in weight per diameter. Modern synthetic lines

are made within extremely close tolerances in this regard. Today's plastic-coated fly lines are also available in a very wide range of weights, colors, styles, and specific gravities that allow the angler to probe all levels of fly-fishable water from the surface down to about 30 feet. They are not susceptible to the ravages of mildew, and the finishes of most are quite long-lasting under normal use.

There are, of course, a few disadvantages to synthetic lines, the main one being that the fibers have a long "memory"—they tend to retain a coiled shape after being left on the reel for a length of time. This necessitates thoroughly stretching the line before fishing, which is a minor bother, but no more so than drying out and dressing a silk line.

As we mentioned in the preceding chapter, present-day American-made fly lines are constructed by applying PVC plastic coatings over braided level-core lines. Floating or sinking is controlled by additives to the coating, which are either of lighter or heavier specific gravity than water, and by the qualities of the core material itself, the specific gravity of Dacron being heavier than water. Braided tapered lines are made in floating, intermediate, slow-sinking, fast-sinking, and extra-fast-sinking versions, as well as in types where only the tip section sinks.

Fly lines made of monofilament came on the scene in recent years. Their main advantage is translucency. Sinking versions are made entirely from mono and cast extremely well. Floating lines are foam-coated over tapered mono cores. In this writer's opinion, their advantages over braided fly lines are not especially noticeable.

Line Weight-Style Coding

American fly-line manufacturers in 1961 adopted a then revolutionary classification system based on the actual weight in grains of the casting portion of the line—which is the front 30 feet excluding any level tip portion.

Under the system adopted by the American Fishing Tackle Manufacturers Association, all fly lines are graded in terms of their weight (from 1-weight to 12-weight). Letter code symbols indicate the taper style and buoyancy qualities. Fig. 13 on the next page illustrates.

When lines were made exclusively with silk cores, they were classified by tip and taper diameters. However, the advent of Dacron and nylon made the system obsolete, because of their

weight differential in relation to natural silk fibers. Early synthetic fly lines identified by the old system caused great confusion and consternation among fly-casters, thus necessitating the development of the AFTMA standards.

Fly-Line Tapers

U.S.-made fly lines come in the seven basic tapers outlined earlier in this chapter.

Level lines are rarely used for casting. Their main function is for trolling flies in lakes and reservoirs. Floating level fly line is also employed as shooting line in conjunction with shooting-head fly lines in sizes ranging from .029 to .035 inch. The main advantage of braided level fly line used this way is that it tends to tangle less than mono and allows the angler to mend his cast, a virtual impossibility with monofilament shooting line.

Double-tapered lines have been the preferred style of most American flyrodders for over a century. The main advantages of the shape lie in its easy controllability at both short and medium distances and the delicacy of presentation that can be achieved with the taper. They are made in both floating and sinking versions.

The double-taper, as it's most often called, may be used in one of two ways.

If you don't anticipate the need for casts over 45 feet, simply cut the double-tapered line in half and splice the large end directly to braided backing line. This allows you to wind onto the reel far more backing than possible when an entire line is used.

If frequent casts over 45 feet are needed, then the angler should probably first splice the front 30 feet or so of the cut line to about 100 feet of 15- to 20-pound-test limp monofilament. The mono is then spliced to the backing line, which in effect converts the double-taper into a shooting head.

Weight-forward fly lines came on the scene in the 1930s under the name "torpedo head." All of the weight-forward tapered line's effective casting weight is concentrated in the front 30 or so feet of the line, which tremendously enhances one's ability to make long-distance casts and to cast highly air-resistant artificials, like bass bugs and steelhead, saltwater, and salmon flies. The remainder of a weight-forward line is fairly small-diameter running line, which serves in a way like the shooting line attached to a shooting head. Weight-forward tapered fly lines are made in floating, sinking, and sinking-tip versions.

Weight code	Weight in grains	Allowable tolerances (in grains)
4	120	114—126
5	140	134—146
6	160	152—168
7	185	177—193
8	210	202—218
9	240	230—250
10	280	270—290
11	330	318—342

Fig. 13. AFTMA fly line weights. Weights are based on the first 30 feet of line, exclusive of any taper or tip. Line weights 1, 2, 3, and 12 are omitted because of their rather limited applications to normal fly-fishing situations. Style code symbols are DT (double-taper), WF (weight-forward), ST (sinking tip), SH (shooting head), SWT (saltwater taper), L (level), and BT (bug taper). AFTMA designations extend only to whether a line floats, sinks, or is of the intermediate type. Some manufacturers, however, designate whether lines are slow-sinking, fast-sinking, or extra-fast-sinking.

Long-belly weight-forward lines are merely weight-forward fly lines with longer-than-normal forward tapers. In most, the belly portion is about 10 feet longer than that of a comparable standard weight-forward taper. The major advantage of the design is that it has some of the better qualities of both double-tapered and weight-forward shapes and, therefore, is more versatile for fishing. When casting at short distances, the long-belly behaves very much like a double-taper. It can be mended, roll-cast, and curve-cast easily. However, once the head of the line is extended to overhang the rod tip a few feet, the line performs much the same as a regular weight-forward taper and can be cast to considerable distances.

Bass-bug tapers and *saltwater tapers* are also weight-forward lines, but in these the casting weight is dramatically concentrated in the business end. This concentration of casting weight is helpful when casting very large, air-resistant artificials. Another quality of the design is that a proficient caster can lift from the water over 60 feet of line into a backcast, then shoot a cast ahead of a cruising gamefish on the next forward rod stroke.

Shooting-taper fly lines (or "shooting heads," as they're commonly called) are approximately 30-foot-long single-tapered lines attached at the butt end to either monofilament or braided level fly line. The remainder of the reel spool is filled with an appropriate amount of 15- to 30-pound-test braided backing line to handle the runs of the gamefish species sought.

A shooting head's main function in fishing is to make long casts with a minimum of effort. It's not needed for fishing unless long-distance casts are the rule rather than the exception.

Fig. 14. Fly-line tapers.

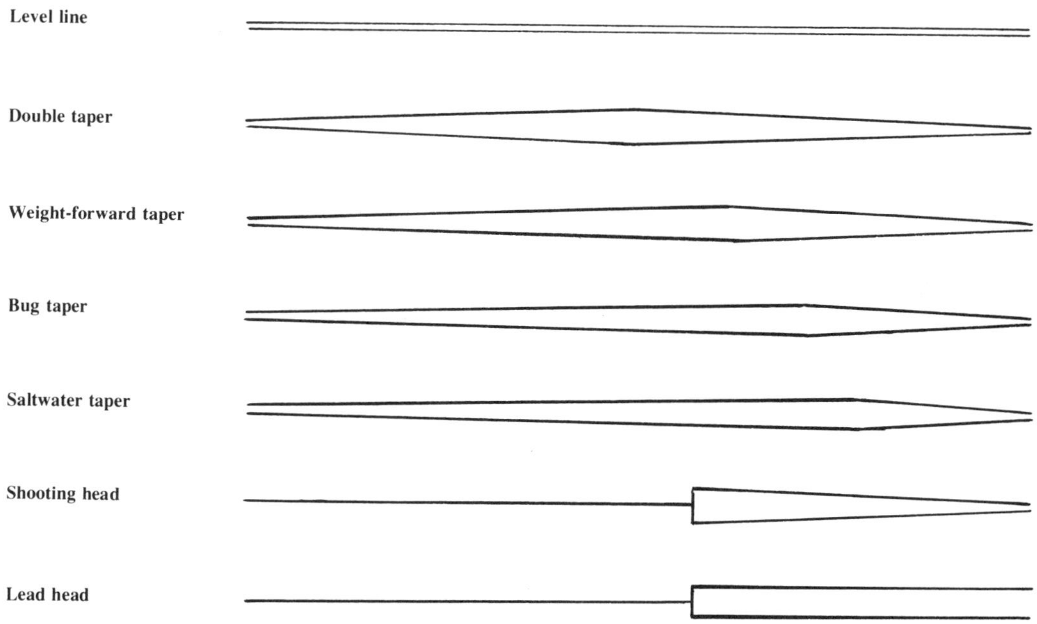

Level line

Double taper

Weight-forward taper

Bug taper

Saltwater taper

Shooting head

Lead head

Fig. 15.   The long-belly weight-forward line is ideal for steelhead and salmon fishing.

Fig. 16.   The shooting head for long casting.

Fig. 17. The double-taper fly line is the correct choice for small to medium-sized streams and delicate presentations.

In tournament casting, the shooting head is a basic tool of certain distance events. More about this in a later chapter.

The cast with a shooting head is made by working the head a few feet past the rod tip with false casts, having previously stripped from the reel enough shooting line to assure the cast reaching its target. The casting stroke incorporates either the single- or double-haul techniques described in Chapters 7 and 8. Casts in fishing situations over 90 feet are possible with shooting-head lines. Casts over 200 feet are possible under tourney conditions.

North American anglers use shooting heads for trout, steelhead, salmon, and saltwater angling. Some, as we mentioned earlier, use a shooting head made from half of a double-tapered fly line. Others purchase factory-made heads which are already cut to proper length and onto which have been spliced braided line loops which are used to attach them to shooting lines.

Spinning, Spin-Casting, and Bait-Casting Lines

Nylon and Dacron synthetic fibers were the technological stepping stones that made possible today's superlative casting lines. The highest-quality mono lines are of remarkable uniformity of strength and diameter from end to end. Monofilament is so controllable a substance that virtually any desired degree of stiffness or limpness can be achieved in its manufacture.

Synthetic-fiber braided casting lines are like-wise outstanding performers. Being less water-absorbent than their silk, linen, and flax predecessors, both nylon and Dacron braided casting lines cling less to the spool after prolonged exposure to water. The light specific gravity of nylon makes possible a floating casting line that requires little or no dressing. Dacron's heavy specific gravity makes possible a sinking casting line that requires no pre-soaking or rubbing down with powdered graphite. Just how good the advanced lines are is attested to by the fact that in the short span of thirty years they've eliminated from competition all lines made from natural fibers.

Properties of Modern Lines

To understand the importance of the line in casting more fully, let's briefly examine those properties which enhance our ability to cast and fish with it. The most important are abrasion resistance, knot strength, limpness, shock resistance, strength, stretch, smoothness, and visibility.

At one time in the not too distant past, it would have been essential to differentiate clearly between lines made for fishing and those braided expressly for the tournament caster. But that's no longer necessary. Most of the lines popular with today's tournament casters are regular fishing lines available from major line manufacturers.

From the caster's point of view, abrasion resistance, knot strength, visibility, and stretch are less important than diameter, limpness, and smoothness. These latter qualities are important to the angler, but after a fish is hooked, the rest also bear upon his ability to land it successfully.

Line strength has a direct bearing on efficient casting with both braided and monofilament lines. The line's tensile strength is the key, for it is the line's break-load per diameter. And what this means to the angler is that the higher the tensile strength of the line, the stronger it is for fishing.

If a line has both high tensile strength and small diameter, it will not only cast farther with less effort as a result of encountering less wind resistance, but it will also help one deal with large gamefish more effectively. More small-diameter line can be packed onto a reel than large-size line. And this can also help handle the big ones.

Limpness can be defined from the dynamics standpoint as the force needed to bend or deflect the line. More force is needed to bend a line of large diameter than one of small diameter. As a result, that part of the large-diameter line in direct contact with the tip guide of the casting rod during the cast is stressed and abraded more than a smaller-diameter line would be.

The primary reason that a degree of limpness is important with open-faced spinning reels is that stiff line tends to balloon off the spool in coils. This increases the chances for snarled line and affects to a noticeable degree one's ability to make long casts. How full the spool is filled with line also affects attainable distance with spinning tackle, but stiffness and limpness are of equal import. Overly limp line won't flow freely off the spool. This affects both distance and accuracy.

The third crucial factor affecting a line's castability is how smoothly it flows through the guides. This quality is less noticeable in monofilament lines than braided ones. To be sure, it is obvious even to the untrained observer that mono is more friction-free than braided line. However, it should be noted that the synthetic fibers have permitted line engineers to braid lines of both very fine diameter and great strength compared to the ones made of silk and linen.

Once the cast is completed, the other qualities assume their roles of relative importance. And the first to be encountered is shock resistance, or the ability of a line to withstand a sudden sharp pull, such as the strike a very heavy fish might put upon it. And this is one area of line design where the stretchiness of the line material assumes some importance. In this case, stretch relates inseparably with shock resistance and limpness. For if the line is not stretchy enough, it will not have enough give to withstand such a shock. On the other hand, if it's too limp and stretchy, the angler may not be able to detect the strike quickly enough to set the hook.

Knot strength is equally crucial to the angling caster. Both the styles of knots and the ways in which they're tied bear upon the line's breaking strength. Most knots tend to weaken any line. For example, ordinary monofilament knotted with an Overhand Knot breaks at about 50 percent of its unknotted strength. By way of contrast, a correctly tied Improved Clinch Knot tests out at up to 100 percent of the unknotted strength of the line. Du Pont's technical experts consider the Overhand Knot the best measure of relative knot strength, because it is the weakest knot that can be tied. They concluded that a line which has a very high Overhand Knot strength is desirable, because it is more forgiving of poorly tied knots. Du Pont formulates their Stren monofilament with this consideration in mind. Stren retains 75 percent or more of its strength when knotted with an Overhand Knot, they claim.

Although there's little evidence to prove that one kind of fishing line frightens a fish more than another, it's been the conclusion of most experienced anglers that certain line and leader materials produce a higher incidence of strikes than others. In a paper presented to the 1972 annual conference of the Outdoor Writers Association of America, Inc., Edwin H. Keller of the plastics department of E. I. du Pont de Nemours & Co., Inc., pointed out that there is no such thing as a completely invisible fishing line. He said that an ideal line would be "completely translucent with a refractive index the same as water," adding that clear nylon monofilament most nearly approaches this ideal. Keller hastened to add, however, that "the slight difference in refraction produces a lens effect and the monofilament will appear dark as the impinging light is directed away from the viewer's eye." This, he said, is heightened when the line is made more opaque by adding a dye or pigment.

Keller said that du Pont researchers undertook a study of line visibility and determined that a fluorescent dye incorporated into the line cancels out the lens effect near the surface and causes the line to blend with the blue-white sky reflections on the surface. Photographic evidence confirmed this conclusion to the researchers' satisfaction, he said. As a result, du Pont incorporated this dye into their Stren and Golden Stren fluorescent fishing lines. Both refract light in the long-wavelength section of the spectrum where the fish's color perception is least responsive, and in colors that are highly visible to the angler above the surface.

Line diameter, of course, is another factor affecting its visibility both above and beneath the surface. And practical experience has proved since Cotton's time that one who fishes as fine as possible has the odds strongly stacked in his favor at the moment the lure or fly swings into a fish's cone of vision.

Each year numerous new monofilament lines reach the angler. Some are claimed to approach the ultimate in invisibility and casting qualities. In some cases, the claims are valid. In others they're not, and the line's performance may fall grossly short of the claims in its behalf.

Although it can be unwise for an author to recommend brand names of fishing lines, particularly monofilament ones whose strength and casting qualities may be influenced by improper storage and age, it would be remiss not to say that if you use fresh shelf-stock lines made by this country's leading manufacturers, chances are they'll not only cast well, but also fish effectively.

Fig. 18.   Six- or 8-pound-test monofilament is just right for handling small lake trout.

Some of the better casting lines made or marketed in this country come from Cortland, du Pont, Ashaway, Garcia, Sunset, Shakespeare, Heddon, Berkeley, Newton, Orvis, and Scientific Anglers/3M. European Kroic and Maxima may also be counted on to perform very well when properly handled and stored.

Which Type of Line for Me?

Both monofilament and braided casting lines may be used effectively on spinning reels of the open-face design. Mono is unquestionably the superior performer for long-distance casting because of its inherent springiness, which prevents it from clinging to the spool.

Ultra-light spinning artists normally choose monofilament lines in the smallest diameters consistent with the fishing conditions. On the other hand, quite a few surf, bass, pike, and muskellunge fishermen definitely prefer braided lines because of their comparative lack of stretch and durability.

The angler really has no choice at all when using a closed-face spin-casting reel. Its line pick-up device won't function satisfactorily with braided line. In addition, the small hole in the reel's nose cone tends to accumulate water picked up by a braided line, which in turn reduces effective casting distance.

Both braided and monofilament lines cast very well on modern, level-wind multiplying bait-casting reels. Here the choice is often most strongly influenced by the average distances to be cast and whether or not the angler wants the line to sink or

Fig. 19. Single-action fly reels come in a wide range of sizes.

float. If a floating line is indicated by the conditions of the moment, say for fishing with floating bass plugs among the lily pads, then waterproofed nylon braided line will undoubtedly be the better choice. But when a deep-running lure like a weighted plastic worm is the object of the fish's affections, then either mono or braided sinking Dacron line may be preferable.

Fly Reels

There are three main types of fly reels in current popular use.

Single-action fly reels are the simplest design of the three and enjoy by far the broadest popularity both here and abroad. Most major U.S. and foreign reel-makers offer one or more single-action reels in their catalogs. Prices range from less than $10 to well over $100.

The conventional single-action reel consists of an open-sided circular frame and spindle, onto which fits a spool that holds the backing line, fly line, and leader. The drag is either a simple click device that works against a toothed gear attached to the interior face of the spool, a pin that mates with a ratchet set into the frame, or one of several kinds of friction drag mechanisms. On better-

Fig. 20. Multiplying fly reels recover line twice as fast as single-action reels.

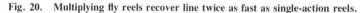

quality reels, the drag is almost always adjustable. One of the most successful reels of this type is the Hardy Featherweight series, for decades the standard of quality among single-action reels for freshwater angling.

Newer more advanced designs have challenged the Featherweight for popularity, however. Some, like Scientific Anglers System reels and Orvis C.F.O. reels, are designed with flanged spools that permit easy finger-braking. Others, like the now discontinued Hardy Perfect and Thompson fly reels, were made so the rotating spool faced on both sides of the reel. This was also a highly desirable feature that permitted easy braking when a fish was on. Currently, both Daiwa and Cortland also offer reels with wraparound spool flanges in lesser price ranges.

When casting and fishing with a single-action fly reel, the line to be cast is pulled off the spool before the cast is made. Prior to the cast, stream fishermen usually coil this line in the hand. After the cast is made and the presentation fished out, some recover the line back in either large or small coils with the line hand. Others retrieve it directly into a stripping basket attached to the waist. Some gather the line into long loops held between their lips. Boat anglers either let it fall in loose loops onto the deck surface or drop it into a pail partly filled with water.

Once a fish takes the fly and the angler sets the hook, the fish is usually permitted to run out the loose line and played off the reel if it's a big one. Tiddlers can be stripped in quickly with medium-length pulls on the line.

Whichever method the angler ultimately decides on to control loose fly line is more or less guided by the fighting qualities of the fish and the length of casts to be made. Casts up to about 50 feet can be made easily with line coiled in the hand. For long-distance casting, a stripping basket belted to the waist or line loops coiled between the lips are preferred. Tournament distance casters arrange their line in long, loose loops directly on the casting platform.

Single-action fly reels are probably the best all-round choice for serious freshwater and marine flyrodders—being available in a very wide selection of sizes to fit rods of all lengths and power potentials.

Multiplying fly reels look very much like single-action ones, externally at least. They're handled in exactly the same ways prior to and following the cast. Internally, however, the multiplying reel is geared to recover line about twice as fast as the single-action model. The advantages are two-

Fig. 21.   An automatic fly reel.

fold. When a fast-moving fish, like an Atlantic salmon, suddenly runs, then changes direction, the multiplying reel lets one recover the slack let into the line very quickly, thereby lessening the chances of losing control over the fish. Another factor in favor of the multiplying reel is that one need turn the handle only half as often in a day's fishing. Now admittedly, this may not seem to be a significant saving of the caster's energy, but it makes quite a difference in how you feel after making several hundred casts and hooking and playing a number of very powerful, strong-running fish.

Automatic fly reels continue to be offered by several old-line American tackle companies. In these, the line is rewound on the spool by depressing a lever with the little finger of the rod hand. This activates a spring-winding mechanism inside the reel housing.

Automatic fly reels have both advantages and shortcomings. Most of them are fairly heavy compared to featherweight single-action and multiplying reels. Few have the line-carrying capacity of the largest-diameter single-action models. And if the reel is accidently dropped into the sand, chances are it will have to be completely disassembled and cleaned before further use. However, when fishing small, brushy creeks for small trout and panfish, the automatic reel saves a lot of time and energy by eliminating the need to turn a handle.

Saltwater fly-fishermen usually prefer special custom-built single-action reels machined from solid bars of corrosion-resistant alloy or coated with finishes that resist saltwater corrosion. These reels often feature disc-type drags engineered to control the runs of the largest, fastest-moving saltwater species, like marlin. Saltwater fly reels range in price from about $20 to $150. And if a fellow is dead serious about fly-rodding for the larger saltwater fishes, it's wise to use the best reel that'll fit the budget. Spindles and drags on freshwater reels simply aren't made to withstand the heat generated by the speedy runs of certain of these fish.

Open-Faced Spinning Reels

Two main types of open-faced spinning reel are presently available to American anglers, the main difference between them being that on skirted-spool versions the spool overlaps the rotor mechanism to prevent line from tangling behind the rotor. This feature is especially helpful when it's windy or the angler is fishing at night.

On all open-faced spinning reels the line is wound on a nonrotating, or fixed, spool. When the cast is made, the line pays off freely from the lip of the spool and is wrapped back onto the spool by a metal bail, a mechanical finger, or a grooved wheel upon which the angler places the line prior to the recovery.

The spool can be adjusted to turn under a given tension to prevent the line from breaking once a fish is hooked. The spool's drag is adjusted by a knurled nut or a thumbscrew that exerts pressure directly against the face of the spool.

Open-faced spinning reels are made in ultra-light-, light-, medium-, and heavy-duty models, as

Fig. 22. An open-faced spinning reel.

well as in freshwater and saltwater types. Those made expressly for saltwater fishing usually have parts made from corrosion-resistant materials, like stainless steel.

Line recovery ratios for open-faced spinning reels vary between 3:1 and 5:1. Reels with slower rates of recovery aren't practical for most fishing situations.

When properly designed and manufactured, a spinning reel is smooth-running, holds adequate line for the fishing to be done, maintains even drag pressure at all settings, and is quiet-running. The gear housing should be tightly sealed against possible entry of foreign matter, like dust and sand.

By far the most popular type of open-face spinning reel in America is the one utilizing a bail pick-up mechanism. Details of its operation will be found in Chapter 12.

Spin-Casting Reels

Spin-casting reels also operate off a fixed spool. But the spool inside the nose cone does not revolve against thumbscrew pressure for braking action. It is truly fixed in its position. Instead, an internal housing containing a retractable pin wraps the line around the spool as the handle is turned. And it is that device which turns to provide controllable braking power.

The better spin-casting reels also oscillate internally so that the pin housing wraps the line in criss-cross fashion on the spool. There was no oscillation on the early spin-casting reels. The line was simply wrapped on the spool to fall as it would, which caused line-jamming when the spool depth was excessive or when very light-test lines were used. And that's why early spin-casting anglers rarely used lines lighter than 6-pound-test.

The spin-casting reel is used very much like the level-wind bait-casting reel. It is affixed to exactly the same kind of offset grip on a bait-casting rod. The basic casting strokes are also the same. However, that's where the similarity ends. The spin-casting reel is possibly the easiest of all casting reels to operate. The level-wind reel is the most difficult.

One of the most useful applications of spin-casting to fishing is in casting weighted plastic worms and spinner baits for bass, pike, and walleye.

Small-sized spin-casting reels of high quality are also excellent for bait-fishing in streams and lakes for trout and panfish. Some will cast baits weighted with only a couple of split shot. Most of the better heavy-duty versions will hold enough line and are strongly enough built to whip down virtually any freshwater gamefish within the limits of their line-carrying capacities, including muskies, northern pike, and lake trout. The tackle isn't very popular with steelhead and salmon fishermen, though. Open-faced reels are preferred for bait and lure drift-fishing because of their very smooth drags and large line capacities.

Fig. 23.   A modern bait-casting reel.

Bait-Casting Reels

Today's multiplying, level-wind bait-casting reels are like fine jeweled watches compared to the primitive centerpin reels of the past. The bait-casting reel is affixed to any of the popular offset casting-rod handles. Although the casting strokes using bait-casting reels are very simple, the thumbing of the spool requires practice to achieve the accuracy and distance of which the equipment is capable.

Modern bait-casting reels are made in models with both regular and fast recovery gear speeds, as well as in versions carrying enough line for surf-casting.

Pfleuger developed its tremendously popular Supreme reel before the First World War. A. F. Meisselbach Mfg. Co., of Elyria, Ohio, also produced a superbly crafted level-wind reel that became popular with tournament casters and anglers. Other excellent reels followed, including those made by Cox, Heddon, South Bend, Hardy Bros., J. W. Young, Daiwa, Abu, and Penn.

The Ambassadeur 5000, 5500, and 6000 series reels, made in Sweden by Abu and distributed in the U.S. by Garcia Corporation, are good examples of the best presently available in level-wind reel design and quality. They offer models in several sizes variously geared for regular or extra-fast line recovery. The Ambassadeur reels also incorporate stardrags, free-spooling that lets one cast without the handle turning, and inertia-inhibiting devices that reduce the chance of backlash. On the Ambassadeur reel, the anti-inertia device consists of two lightweight fiber governors forced outward on needlelike shafts to exert pressure against the reel frame.

The purpose of the level-wind feature, of course, is simply to wrap the line evenly on the spool. On early-day reels lacking this feature, the angler had to guide the line onto the spool with his thumb and index finger.

Level-wind bait-casting reels are ideally suited to handling outsized gamefish like steelheads, lake trout, muskellunge, northern pike, and the various ocean surf species. They will accommodate both braided and monofilament lines, though the mono makes possible longer casts.

About the lightest practical casting weight for use with a medium-action bait-casting rod of moderate stiffness is ⅜ ounce. Light-action bait-casting rods will handle lures down to about ¼ ounce. Lures lighter than ¼ ounce are best cast with open-faced spinning tackle.

Chapter 3

Terminal Tackle

Terminal tackle is probably most often defined as the *total assembly* affixed to the end of the casting line, rather than any of its single components, such as the leader, bobber, hook, bait, fly, sinker, or lure. Thus, when we refer to terminal tackle for spinning, we may be describing one of a large number of possible rigs. The terminal tackle for lure-fishing for trout may be nothing more than a simple wobbling spoon. On the other hand, it may be a fairly complex rig consisting of several items, such as a bobber, sliding plastic beads, a split shot, a hook, and a live insect nymph, like a hellgrammite.

Terminal tackle for tournament casting usually consists of nothing more than a leader to which is knotted either a fly or a weighted casting plug.

Leaders

Leaders for fly- or bait-casting are nowadays almost exclusively made from the various kinds of monofilament materials, with the obvious exception of steel-cored leaders used to fish for sharp-toothed gamefish like pike. Bait-casting leaders are almost always made in level, unknotted form. Level fly-fishing leaders became obsolete decades ago. Modern-day flyrodders use either knotless or knotted tapered leaders in a wide variety of lengths, colors, and tapers.

There are arguments favoring both knotless and knotted fly-fishing leaders, but the knotless versions present a couple of incontestable advantages: they won't grab pieces of weed or flotsam, and they are stronger from end to end than those with knotted sections.

Factory-made tapered leaders are available in both hard- and soft-monofilament types. Dry-fly anglers usually prefer the hard mono, because of the excellent leader turnover to be achieved with leaders made from it. Nymph and streamer fishermen gravitate more toward soft mono tippets attached to hard mono butt sections. Some prefer the entire leader to be tapered from the softer material, because it enhances the mobility of flies swum under the influences of current and retrieve.

Baits

Live baits used for casting include a tremendous variety of living aquatic and terrestrial insects, arthropods, cephalopods (squids), and annelids (worms and leeches). Some of the more popular baits for freshwater fishing include angleworms, nightcrawlers, shiners, dace, chubs, smelts, hellgrammites, dragonfly nymphs, grasshoppers, crickets, shrimps, and crayfish. Some of the most popular live baits for saltwater angling are herring, sand shrimps, sand crabs, anchovies, clams, mussels, and squids. Both freshwater and saltwater anglers frequently trim-cut or fillet baitfish in order to make them behave in an enticing manner in the water. Baitfish so altered are usually referred to as cut baits.

The variety of popular artificial baits in current use is even longer than that of preferred live baits. It includes cured single salmon eggs and dead minnows, frozen salmon egg roe, cured salmon egg skeins, pork-rind strips, cheese baits, miniature marshmallows, pork chunks, plastic worms and eels, rubber or plastic fishes or squids, plastic insects and frogs. Some artificial baits, like pork-rind chunks, are heavy enough to cast without adding sinkers to the line or leader. This also

Fig. 24. Live, cured, or artificial baits are often highly effective on large freshwater fishes.

Fig. 25.   An outsized spinner-caught whitefish.

they're made in dozens of shapes, weights, and sizes. Unlike spinners, the wobbling spoons' actions in the water are erratic; they swing back and forth horizontally when retrieved.

Plugs

Plugs are wooden or plastic lures to which are sometimes attached wobbling or spinner devices to impart additional fish-enticing flash or action. Some plugs are made expressly to be fished on the surface. Others are designed to probe either intermediate or extreme depths. Still others are made to perform their deadliest dances when trolled at steady speeds. Plugs are made in a tremendous variety of shapes, weights, and color combinations to resemble small aquatic animals and fishes, terrestrial creatures like frogs and mice, and arthropods like crayfish.

Feathered Lures

Feathered lures are sold under quite a few varietal names, including jigging flies, jigging lures, jigs, go-getters, and a host of others.

Essentially, a feathered lure is a weighted or unweighted hook to which has been attached feathers. Saltwater anglers normally refer to feathered lures simply as feathers. Feathered jigging lures are normally lead-weighted hooks to which are wrapped various colors of feather, hair, or Mylar. They're normally fished by casting them out and bouncing them along the bottom or by retrieving them through the water. They're also fished effectively by fishing them on sliding or fixed bobber rigs.

Flies

Artificial flies are feathered lures that are designed expressly to be fished on fly-fishing tackle. They fall into four basic groupings: dry flies, which are made to imitate floating insects; wet and nymph flies, which are dressed to resemble drowned or immature aquatic insects; streamer and bucktail flies, which suggest minnow life; and popping bugs, which suggest creatures like frogs and mice, or injured baitfish like sardines.

holds true of certain live baits, like small squids and fishes.

Spinners

Spinners fall into the category of artificial lures. They consist of polished, hammered, satin-finished or painted metal or plastic blades that revolve around wire shafts or from swivels.

The flashing of a spinner's blade (or blades) is assumed to attract certain predatory fish because of its resemblance to the light refracted off the scales of living baitfish and other aquatic food organisms. Possibly the sonic disturbance the spinner creates while rotating in the water also helps attract fish.

Wobbling Spoons

Wobbling spoons derive their name from the fact that the earliest ones were made from eating utensils with the handles cut off. Like spinners,

Chapter 4

Rod and Casting Dynamics

In order to cast effectively—to deliver the casting weight with authority and accuracy over a wide range of distances—it's very important to glean an understanding of the physical forces governing bodies in motion.

Simply stated, casting is the act of propelling the weight of a fly line or a lure (also referred to here as the casting weight) with some sort of casting instrument, which is most correctly called a rod.

(In America at least, one occasionally hears a casting rod called a pole. Strictly speaking, within the tolerable ambiguities of the English language, a fishing rod may be correctly referred to as a pole. But in the common usage of the angling fraternity, a pole more properly is a still-fishing rod—usually an unjointed whole bamboo cane—to the extreme end of which is knotted a length of fishing line. In this book, therefore, all casting instruments will be referred to as rods.)

To be sure, it's possible to make fishing casts of considerable distance and accuracy without the aid of a rod at all. This is done by manipulating a fly line with the hands and arms, or by swinging and releasing weighted lures attached to free casting line. However, fly-casting without a rod is essentially a trick used by casting instructors to demonstrate the effect of line speed. It's not an easy exercise to perform and is well beyond the abilities of the average tyro caster.

"Hand-casting" with plugs once enjoyed a degree of popularity here in the United States. It still does in parts of Scandinavia. But American anglers no longer consider the technique especially sporting, so we won't deal with it further.

Needless to say, the study of casting dynamics—which is the study of a cast lure or fly line in motion—can be just as involved as the student

caster wants to make it, in that it deals primarily with the laws of physics. But from the angling caster's point of view at least, the more abstruse aspects are more academic than practical when it comes to catching fish. On the other hand, the serious tournament caster will find that an intensive study of the theory of kinetic energy and how it applies to casting is helpful, because the objective in that situation is to perfect each facet of one's technique to the utmost, much in the same way a tournament-circuit golf pro works on his game.

So what we'll do here is outline certain of the most important principles governing casting and casting equipment, and describe them in the simplest lay terminology consistent with clarity and technical accuracy. When the precise language of the physicist must be used, the terminology will be painstakingly defined and illustrated with clarifying analogies and examples. By using this approach, an attempt will be made to strike some sort of acceptable middle ground that will neither confuse the beginner nor bore the more advanced caster. I hope this chapter will satisfy and enlighten both in their passionate search for ways to become more proficient at the rewarding sport of angling.

Rod Design

The rod itself is made up of one or another kind of fiber-to-matrix combination, including split-cane rods, which are of solid construction. Bamboo is a natural fiber in a natural pith matrix. A glass rod is a combination of glass fibers in a resin matrix material. Graphite rods are made of graphite fibers in a resin matrix similar to that used to

Fig. 26.   A rod's qualities and performance are definable.

bind together fiberglass fibers. In a boron rod, the fibers consist of boron crystals adhering to minute tungsten wires. These strands also are held together by a resin matrix. What the matrix material does is hold everything together so that as one fiber is stressed, its load is transferred to the fiber next to it, and so on, thereby storing energy.

In essence, then, a rod is a total structural commodity. And therefore, from an engineering standpoint, can be defined as a structure, which in this case is a *cantilever beam.*

A bamboo rod happens to be a four-, five-, or six-sided cantilever beam once it's shaped and glued into rod sections. A glass rod is a cantilever beam that's either solid in construction or formed into a hollow, tapered tube.

The properties of a cantilever beam are made up of *mass, moment of inertia* (what happens to the mass off the central axis), and the *strength-strain capability* of the basic material. Strength is important so that the rod will resist breaking when it's bent on top. Strain enters the picture because it involves the compressibility or stretch of the material. And from this threefold relationship of inertia, mass, and stretch-strain, one gets the *effective stiffness* of the rod. That's what all

rod-builders work with—effective stiffness—which is not a pure materials category.

Aerospace technicians coined a new name—*modulus*—to describe the resistance to bending of various materials. However, it's important to remember that modulus is a pure *materials* word. It refers to the material's stiffness. And essentially, what the caster needs to know about modulus is that the higher the modulus of a material, the less of it is needed to duplicate a given stiffness profile. This means that with high-modulus materials, some real power potential can be packed into a rod without a resulting increase in rod weight or diameter. The term *specific modulus* refers to the rod's stiffness per given defined cross-section. By way of explanation, if you have materials that are the same, and take a square cantilever beam and a round, hollow one, the modulus of those materials is the same, but the specific modulus is different. Specific modulus is used in two ways—both relatively confusing to the layman. One is to divide the modulus itself by the specific gravity of the material so that you derive a stiffness-per-unit weight. The other is a specific modulus that's used in reference to area cross-section and type of cross-section. In this case one says simply: "The specific modulus of a round versus a square tapered cross-section of a rod is . . ."

Neither means much to the caster. What's really important to him is the rod's flexibility, stiffness, and ability to load and recover. These are the qualities which help the layman understand what a rod's going to do.

For example, take a hollow, round, tapered tube made out of one layer of a given material which has a given modulus, a given strength, a given strain, and a given stiffness. Now if you take the same amount of material and roll it onto a 1-inch-diameter mandrel, then the resulting rod will have a wall thickness that's so much, a diameter that's so much, and a given stiffness.

Take that same amount of material and roll it over a ½-inch mandrel and you'll have more than one layer. It too will have its own flexural capabilities and effective stiffness, but they'll be different than those of the 1-inch-diameter rod. The amount of material that's in the rod's wall, the diameter, and the taper—these are the elements that *define* the rod.

From a layman's standpoint, he picks up a rod and waggles it, and what he feels and sees—how much glass is in the wall, how big the diameter is, and how the diameter changes over the rod's length—are what count. That's all.

Take for example the Phillipson Scotchply rod. The modulus of the Scotchply material is 3.9. The modulus of a Scientific Anglers rod is 4.2. These are pure numbers and relative to the actual constructed material. They are derived in a number of ways: three-point loading (or, the resistance to bending which is the modulus); by means of a straight pull; and by the materials' resistance to stretch. But this is a purely theoretical definition of the materials.

What's important is that a rod-builder can take a 3.9-modulus material, a 4.2-modulus material, and a 4.5-modulus material, and by defining the diameter, the wall thickness, and the taper, construct three rods that are exactly the same in action.

So, from the engineering standpoint, it isn't modulus that the caster is really buying. Modulus is merely part of what makes up the structural quality of the rod. *Flexural strength* and *tensile strength* also affect its structural quality.

The flexural strength of a hollow, round rod can be defined by a mathematical engineering formula. And what it takes into consideration is the diameter, wall thickness, and basic strength of the material.

Taper also affects a rod's structural qualities. The diameter changes in a rod from end to end, but the material supposedly doesn't change. However, in effect, it does change. There isn't as much material at the butt as at the tip. The tip may have four wraps of material and the butt only three. And all of this is constantly changing because of the rod's taper.

Flexure and *effective stiffness* are tied into the design as well. And without going into the formulas, all that the rod designer can really come back to is that the definition of the taper, wall thickness, and diameter determines it. Because the material for the rod has been designed into it to feel right, he can make the same rod out of a number of different materials by changing these three elements. As a result, there are numerous good rods on the market that all have the same general appearance, but differing *personalities*—because great rod designers like Lou Stoner, Jim Green, Bill Phillipson, and the late Jon Tarantino in effect have said: "I want this rod to react in a certain way." They defined, in turn, the materials from which the rods were made, planed and glued split-cane sections or laid fiberglass onto a mandrel of a certain taper in a certain way—and that was it, a great rod!

Rod-Building Materials

Split-cane rods have longitudinal fibers that run right through the nodes, although the fibers are disrupted somewhat there and at the ferrules. The fiber concentration at the outer surface of Tonkin cane is much more dense than at the inner surface. The pith, or matrix material, holds all the bamboo fibers together.

Bamboo is light and very powerful because of this high outside fiber concentration. In the raw cane form, it's also very weather-resistant.

From a design standpoint, whether the cane rod is four-, five-, or six-sided doesn't really make any difference. What the rod designer works with is the fiber density and fiber strength of the bamboo material. The rod's action and stiffness are built in by its butt diameter and taper. But the fact that the cross-section of a bamboo rod is not uniform makes it a very difficult engineering material to analyze and categorize, although the structure once put together can be analyzed. The bamboo rod builder sets up a rough pattern, builds a prototype rod, and casts with it. If it feels right and casts properly, then that's the beginning of a new design.

Fig. 27.   Tacking fiberglass to the mandrel.

Most of the glass rods built out of woven fiberglass cloth are formed by wrapping variously shaped lengths of the material around tapered steel mandrels. The cloth is impregnated with a particular resin system before it's wrapped on the mandrel. The next step consists of wrapping the resined cloth with one of several types of cellophane. The rod is then cured in a large oven, removed from the mandrel, ground and polished, mounted with a grip, reel seat and guides, and finally finished with one of several kinds of suitable varnishes, plastic coatings, or resins.

The main differences between rods made of fiberglass cloth are in the various resin systems used by the manufacturers. Other factors affecting the rod's ultimate quality include the cure cycle, laminating pressure, and quality control.

Epoxy, polyester, and phenolic resin systems are the main bonding agents currently in use. Of the three, in terms of relative quality and efficiency, the epoxy systems probably rank only slightly above the polyesters. At one time almost all rodmakers used phenolic resins as fiberglass bonding agents. But phenolic resins are extremely gaseous

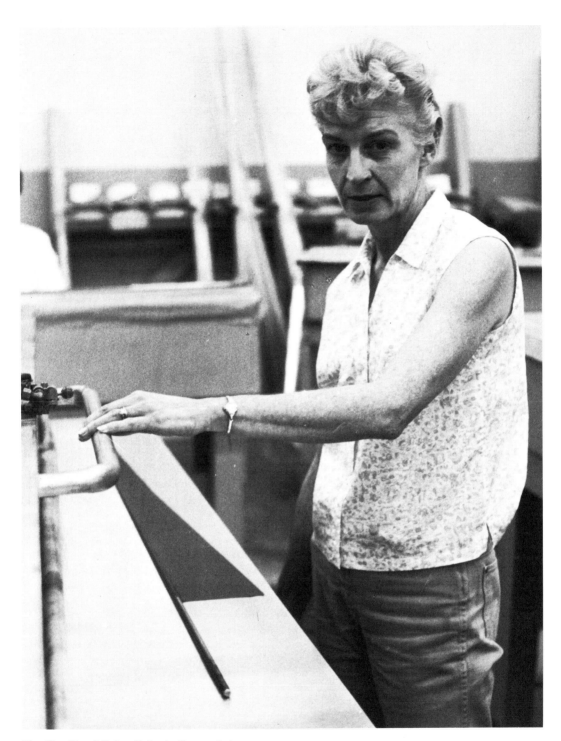

Fig. 28. The cloth is rolled onto the mandrel.

Fig. 29. Cellophane is wrapped on the resined cloth.

and difficult to use. They also have a tendency to crystallize in time, so as the rod is used by flexing, the laminations tend to start working against themselves after prolonged use, thereby limiting the effective casting life of the rod.

The objective of most rod-makers is to design rods that will carry the casting weight—to release energy to the casting weight or fly line gently but powerfully. If, for example, only the *middle* of the rod is loaded, then only a certain amount of energy can be stored in and released by the rod. If the tip is made stiff, the resulting rod will cause the caster problems forming a good fly-casting loop. If the rod is made too flexible, the caster will also have line loop and control problems. On the other hand, if the rod tends to work throughout its length, then it follows that energy is stored in it all the way from the tip to the butt. And here is where rod-builders are forced to make one of the many compromises inherent to their science.

The average caster has to create a timing between his arm, wrist, elbow, shoulder, and muscle tone in order to cast effectively with any rod. And it's demonstrable that most people cast somewhat better with quick rods than with soft, slow ones.

To digress only slightly, graphite rods are interesting in this regard because they are very stiff and, as a result, very quick. That makes them fairly easy to cast. But the average caster wants *three* things in a rod: quickness, fishability, and feel. His needs are far more complex than those of the tournament caster whose main requirement is castability—power plus lack of torque. And it's a quality of advanced materials like graphite, boron, and unidirectional Scotchply to noticeably enhance feel. This can be demonstrated by running the tip of a rod made from one of those substances across a rough surface, then repeating the experiment with a rod made from woven fiberglass cloth.

Rods made from unidirectional fibers also allow the caster to load energy into the rod and get it back out more productively. And that's why all the current interest in advanced materials.

According to Fenwick's president, Phil Clock, graphite is not a good rod-building material unless the manufacturer knows how to make a good rod. He says:

I think that one thing graphite does for us, and the problem it solves, is that we can do things which are beyond the capabilities of other materials. We can achieve what we want to in the way of a design and still have a structurally sound casting tool. And you can't do that with fiberglass. . . . We have made fiberglass rods that are the equivalent of the graphite rods as far as

Fig. 30.   The rods are cured in large ovens.

Rod-Building Materials   51

casting properties. They're very large in diameter and very, very thin-walled. We feel that .020-inch wall thickness is minimum for strength. And these have wall thicknesses down around .012-inch . . . there was no way we could ever market them. It was a kind of prototype deal that didn't work out.

Clock says the graphite rods have significant wall thickness—about .030 inch—and they have ample strength in them to take the beating that a fisherman will give them.

Michael M. Stocker, head of the California Tackle Company, the firm that produces the Sabre fiberglass rods, isn't as optimistic about present-day graphite rods as Clock.

I can only voice a personal opinion that I don't think there's a place in fishing rods for graphite. I don't think that graphite will withstand the abuse that fiberglass will. Because of the modulus of graphite, it only has a fraction of the flex. It would require a completely new educational program for people who are accustomed to pulling up a rod real fast, or for people who are accustomed to bringing it back in order to get to a fish. The fracture of graphite is much lower than that of fiberglass by virtue of the fact that the fibers in fiberglass stretch, where they don't in graphite.

The only area that I think it has some real potential is in the fly-rod area, because here you have much better control, and because of the quick recall of the graphite fibers, you're going to get greater distance. You won't get as much flex back, but it will give more of a snap apparently, which tends to throw the line out. And because you don't have as much flex back, you have less room for error. The tip of the rod isn't floating as much. So you can certainly control your accuracy and distance much better with graphite than you can with fiberglass.

Stocker says that the longer fly rods in the 8- to 9-foot class were the ones they had found most effective in graphite versions. His prediction is:

I think that in the final development of graphite, you're going to find that graphite is going to be effective, but it's not going to be used as it's being presented today. It's going to be used as a *hybrid*—a combination of glass and graphite. Graphite will be used to achieve lesser weight, but the combination is going to be the answer.

Stocker isn't alone in this opinion, either. Other prominent researchers, like Cecil E. Jacobs, laboratory supervisor of 3M's Leisure Time Products and New Business Ventures Division, projects that the rod of the future will be made of composite/composite materials—hybrid rods made essentially from a marriage of fiberglass, boron, and graphite fibers. It's Jacobs' belief that tomorrow's casting instruments will find boron, graphite, and fiberglass fibers each in the right places in the rod structure and that there will probably be a *gradation* of material away from and around the mandrel.

Jacobs says that this will result in a fishing rod that has very nearly the same kind of feel and action as present-day rods. But he says the space-age rod will have the ability to make longer casts. However, it's Jacobs' opinion that some of the castability of current graphite rods will be traded off for fishability. Sensitivity, he says, will be greatly enhanced. The hybrid rods will be basically "better glass rods," possessing all the toughness, durability, and brute force of present-day fiberglass casting instruments, plus the great qualities of feel inherent to rods of unidirectional fiber construction.

However, in this writer's opinion and that of certain designers, it's questionable whether or not the hybrid rods will be superior overall to those made of split cane. Undoubtedly they will be better than today's glass rods for castability and much more sensitive than everything other than all-graphite, Scotchply, and split cane. They'll very likely have better fishability than the current advanced composite rods, but less fishability than present-day tubular glass rods.

Tournament casters of future generations will probably lean strongly toward all-graphite or all-boron rods. Their needs are less demanding in terms of adaptability, and thus require fewer trade-offs that might sacrifice casting power. Graphite will be an ideal rod material for the tournament distance and accuracy casters, in that they'll be able to get the needed distances with greater accuracy—because of the very qualities that work against graphite as a good *fishing* rod material.

In any case, the future is rosy for both fishermen and tournament casters.

Casting Factors

Now let's discuss the laws of nature that govern the ability to make effective casts.

To begin with, all activities involving propelling a fly line or a casting weight are governed by the physical laws of kinetic energy, which is that form of energy possessed by a body by virtue of its motion. In the study of kinetic energy's influence on casting, there are a number of factors to consider. These include inertia, momentum, velocity, gravitational force, air resistance, wind, the qualities of the casting instrument, and the caster's physical strength.

Of these factors, velocity is the most important. The initial problem of the caster is to put the weight of the fly line or fishing lure into motion. In order to do this, it's necessary first to overcome the initial inertia of that weight and somehow impart momentum to it. Inertia is the tendency of a body to remain at rest or resist being put into motion. (Quantitatively, momentum is the product of a body's linear velocity and its mass.)

Once the casting weight has momentum, it also has velocity, which is a vector quantity—one totally specified by both a magnitude and a direction. The direction of the cast may be linear or angular. And in casting, one of the limiting factors is that velocity cannot be maintained absolutely constant, because of the effects of gravity and air resistance.

Gravity imparts a downward force which causes a falling object to accelerate at a hair less than 32 feet per second. Air resistance increases as the square of the velocity approaches the weight of the casting weight, which is called the point of limiting velocity by physicists. In the case of gravity's effect on the casting weight, a point of limiting velocity also is reached as the cast approaches its outer limits.

So what we're really saying is that when we make a cast, the casting weight propelled at an angle from the horizontal plane is actually influenced by both horizontal and vertical velocities.

The magnitude of casting velocity simply consists of the speed of the casting weight. And lure or line speed is achieved in several ways. One method is to exert a relatively weak force to the weight over a long period of time. Another is to apply conservative force over a moderate period of time. Still another is to concentrate great force within a very brief period of time. Each method of developing velocity can result in generating an equal amount of energy at the weight at the precise moment it's released from the rod. And for this reason, it's possible for a caster of limited physical strength to equal in distance casts made by more powerful individuals. This is done by applying force to the rod over a wider arc than that needed by the strong-armed chap.

You may recall that we mentioned earlier in the chapter that the inertia of the casting weight is overcome and momentum generated in it by applying energy to the rod. The source of this energy is the caster's hand. Applying energy to the rod causes it to flex like a spring, store energy in the fibers, then release the energy (which is sometimes referred to as rod thrust) as the rod snaps back to its original shape.

Velocity, in turn, is imparted to the casting weight by concentrating the energy generated by the various body movements into rapidly accelerating strokes which cause the rod to flex, store the energy, then release it very suddenly.

The velocity needed to accomplish a given cast may be very high, as in the case of making a long cast with heavy surf-casting tackle which utilizes several ounces of lead as a casting weight. It may also be very low, such as when making a 25-foot cast with a light-action fly rod. So ultimately, what both fishing and tournament casters try to do is effectively impart velocity to the casting weight over the widest possible range of climatic conditions and within the limitations imposed by both the tackle and their physical strength.

Wind is probably the most troublesome of the limiting factors influencing the cast. Because the direction and force of wind are completely beyond one's control, as they are in golf or tennis, the caster tries to adapt his techniques to make the best of the highly varied conditions brought about by moving air.

For example, a strong wind from any direction will have a marked effect on attainable line speed or velocity. A wind driving down from the caster's rear may in fact enhance his ability to make long casts. But if it quarters in from either side, or blows directly into his face, it may be necessary for him to impart greater line/lure velocities than would normally be needed to deliver that cast in dead air over the same distance. Wind may also force the caster to adjust the arc described by the line or lure one way or another from what might normally be considered ideal.

The Importance of the Rod

Although the role of the casting rod can't be discounted in terms of the amount of energy it can store and release, some anglers tend to place more importance on rods than they deserve. Like any other mechanical tool, a rod's potential is measurable, and once determined, entirely predictable. Several factors contribute to this.

The first rod quality we'll examine is the rate of recovery—or, how fast or slow a rod returns to its original shape after being bent like a spring and released. Both the qualities of the rod material and the way it is placed within the rod structure affect the rod's recovery speed and stiffness.

Like any spring, each rod has a given rate at which it does its work. This may vary considerably between individual rods. Also like a spring, a rod vibrates up and down a certain number of times per second when bent and released. The rate of these vibrations and the rod's inherent potential are determined by the characteristics of the material, as we mentioned earlier. This speed of vibration remains constant in a rod until additional weight is added to it at any point along its length. Adding weight causes a measurable reduction in the vibration speed. The farther toward the unattached end of the rod the added weight is placed, the greater is the reduction in vibration speed, or damping, as it's called.

Rod Actions

Rod actions of various stiffness are obtained by varying the taper or tubular cross-section, weight placement of the material, and by the weight and placement of handles, grips, reel seats, guides, and wrappings.

Split-cane rods have *fast* damping qualities, which are particularly desirable in fly rods. That's because excessive rod-tip vibration causes a fly line to flow out in wavy loops which work against both distance and accuracy.

The rod's recovery rate influences the speed it can impart to the casting weight and, in the case of fly-casting, the relative wideness of the line loop. A very narrow line loop enhances one's ability to make long casts. That's because the relatively small surface it presents to the air encounters less air resistance than a wide loop. Narrow line loops and long casts with fly rods are most easily accomplished with rods having quick recovery and good damping qualities.

The loading qualities of a rod are also very important, that is to say how much weight is required to bend the rod to where it can store energy. And here is where the balance between a fly rod and fly line enters the picture.

Balance

In a nutshell, all rods deliver their stored energy most efficiently under the influence of specific amounts of casting weight. Casting weight is expressed in ounces or fractions thereof in the case of lures, plugs and baits. Under the simplified line-weight designation system of the American Fishing Tackle Manufacturers Association (AFTMA), the weights of fly lines are expressed in grains. The weighed portion of the line is its front 30 feet, excluding any level tip section.

If the casting weight is too heavy for a given rod, its rate of recovery will be too slow to impart the stored-up energy efficiently. If the casting weight is too light for that rod, its deflection will be insufficient to store adequate energy to make a good cast. In either case, the end result is a loss of some much-needed stored energy and, in turn, less velocity than may be needed to accomplish the cast. This principle applies to rods built of split-cane, fiberglass, carbon-graphite, or boron.

A good example of the effects of loading a rod with weight is found in the differences between split-cane and fiberglass rods. A bamboo rod will bend to a specific point, beyond which the cane fibers will break. Such a break may be caused by trying to cast a weight that's too heavy for the rod, by applying too much force to the rod, or by a combination of both.

Certain fiberglass rods, on the other hand, can be bent from tip to butt without overstressing the fibers. At first consideration, this might seem to be a desirable quality in a fishing rod. To be sure, it has been used at times as a selling point in favor of glass rods over those made from split cane. But how far a rod flexes means little when one is concerned primarily with casting a rod to which line or lure weight is balanced to bring out its best casting qualities, or when designing a rod with reasonably similar action over a wide range of casting distances—which is really what rod-building is all about.

Learning How to Cast Well

The theory of casting may at first seem fairly simple—parallel in ways to how golf theory seems easy to one who has never hit a golf ball—but what seems theoretically very simple often turns into massive frustration in practice.

That isn't to say casting is either as difficult or demanding a sport as golf. It isn't, in most instances. The arc described by the rod tip is somewhat shorter than that of the club head and therefore requires a shorter span of directional control. But effective casting requires practice, the same *quality* of practice needed to become a low-handicap golfer. And the serious angler will accept this reality cheerfully if he wants to perfect his skills above pedestrian levels.

The key to this is learning how to compress and release the energy imparted to the casting rod efficiently and with control. And that's what the instructional chapters to follow will attempt to illustrate.

Chapter 5

The Casting Games

Why Casting Games?

Although there are a lot of individual reasons why anglers practice and compete with one another at casting, the underlying purpose of it all is to improve one's ability to catch fish. To be sure, there's a tremendous amount of pleasure to be gained from bettering the distance or accuracy scores of other casters. The same is true concerning the sports of competitive rifle, pistol, or shotgun shooting. But what the casting games are really intended for is to teach one how to select and use balanced tackle effectively.

As the American Casting Association states in its official rule book: "Casting hookless plugs and flies at targets, on land or water, or tournament casting, is a very sorry substitute indeed for the pursuit of fish in their natural habitat." But although the games have had their ups and downs over the years, they remain the best way yet discovered for an angler to perfect his casting skills to the utmost of his ability.

History of the Games in America

The earliest organized casting tournaments held in this country were conducted near Syracuse, New York, in the 1870s. One of the foremost casters of that time was Seth Green of the Onondaga Lake Club, for whom a famous fly is named. The first fly-casting games in the New York City area were held at Coney Island in June 1881, under the sponsorship of the Association for the Protection of Fish and Game. Another caster of repute was Ruben Wood (for whom another famous fly is named). The first tournament held by the National Rod and Reel Association was conducted in Central Park in New York City in 1882.

At first, all events were fly-casting distance tests. They were scored on the threefold basis of distance, accuracy, and delicacy of presentation.

Bait-casting events entered the games in 1884 under the category of minnow-casting. The casting weights for this event were ½-ounce sinkers. Surf-casting was also popular in that era, but a tournament event for surf tackle was cast only once, under the sanction of the organization that was eventually to become the National Association of Scientific Angling Clubs.

Short bait-casting rods were also products of those times. They originated in Kalamazoo, Michigan. And for a long time, the short rods were referred to as Kazoo rods, in honor of the city of their origin. Unlike the earlier bait-casters who used long rods and slung the weight, casters of the Kazoo rods used multiplying reels and threw the weight.

Casting games suffered some loss of popularity in the East during the late 1880s, a victim of the ascendency of both cycling and boating. But they were catching on in the Western U.S. In 1891, the Chicago Fly Casting Club was formed and sponsored a tournament at the World's Columbia Exposition in the "windy city." The events held there were in both expert and amateur classes. They consisted of long-distance fly-casting, distance and accuracy fly-casting, accuracy and delicacy fly-casting and bait-casting accuracy and distance events. Roll-casting for accuracy was also included.

Standardization of casting events began about 1900 at the Third Open to the World tournament in Chicago. And in 1901, the American Fly Casters Association was created to formulate rules governing fly-casting events, which ultimately included distance, dry-fly, roll-casting, obstacle casting, and light-rod categories.

The 1905 Chicago-sponsored tournament was the first tourney in the U.S. specified as an international event. Clubs from San Francisco, Chicago, Grand Rapids, Kalamazoo, Fox River Valley, Racine, Illinois, and Kansas City participated. Anglers Club tournaments began in New York City the following year.

Kalamazoo's First Open Tournament, held in 1905, included a ladies' event. It was also at this gathering that a new national bait- and fly-casting association was formed. This organization became the National Association of Scientific Angling Clubs following the 1906 meet.

By this time, the tournament games included events for salmon professional, salmon amateur, roll-casting, light-tackle distance fly, heavy-tackle distance fly, single-hand fly distance, fly delicacy and accuracy, and bass fly. Bait-casting events included minnow, lure accuracy, ¼-ounce accuracy, ½-ounce accuracy, and ½-ounce distance.

The NASAC retained its name for the next thirty years, and in 1910 a foreign rod won an event for the last time.

"Professionalism" in casting was first defined in 1913. The national Amateur Casting Association was formed in 1913 because professionalism and coincident commercialism had crept into the sport, and many casters felt the need for an amateur organization. However, the casting games themselves were the same as those cast under NASAC rules.

Dry-fly tournament casting got its start in 1916 at the 250th Anniversary Celebration of Newark, New Jersey. This was the final year for heavy- and light-tackle distance fly events. Fishermen's plug games were also tried that year in both accuracy and distance categories.

Then came World War I. During the first year of the war there was no NASAC tourney. However, some tournaments started in the northwestern region of the nation.

By 1918, fifteen events were included on most club schedules, and by 1936, the official dry fly was adopted. In 1939 the association reincorpo-

rated in Ohio as the National Association of Angling and Casting Clubs. It was during that mid-1930 period, which has come to be known as the golden age of casting, that Marvin Hedge and Richard G. Miller shattered existing 5¾-ounce fly-rod distance records with casts of 147 feet and 183 feet respectively. By 1943 the ⅝-ounce bait-casting distances soared to over 400 feet; early-day efforts were only slightly more than half that distance.

Today, the amateur caster's regulatory body is the American Casting Association, which lists eight freshwater accuracy casting games. Five are plug events. ACA recognizes three fly accuracy games and further categorizes them as ACA Official, Skish, and Special events.

The official games were created years ago for competitive purposes and endure to this day with changes reflecting technological advances in tackle. Skish events are more recent. They were introduced in the 1940s under the sponsorship of tackle manufacturers and were originally intended to be games in which *fishing* tackle only would be used, in contrast to the highly specialized equipment then in vogue for tournament casting. Today, with the significant improvements in fishing tackle being what they are, most competitors use tackle permissible for Skish in the Official events.

The ACA publishes official rules and descriptions of each of the accuracy casting events in their publication, *Tournament Fly and Bait Casting Guide*.

Another fast-growing national organization, the Federation of Fly Fishermen, conducts three casting games that relate well to actual fly-fishing conditions. Their Trout Fly Game restricts all casters in the event to a lightweight rod that balances with a double-tapered 6-weight fly line. It is somewhat comparable to the Skish fly event of the ACA. The FFF Bass Bug Game, in which rods up to 9¼ feet long and 9-weight bass-bug-taper lines are used, and the FFF Angler Distance Game, in which a 300-grain shooting head backed with 20-pound-test flat mono shooting line is required, are both gaining popularity among the federation's associated clubs.

Chapter 6

Basic Fly-Casting

Assembling the Tackle

Fly-casting equipment must be correctly assembled to function properly during the casting strokes. The elements to be assembled and balanced include the rod itself, the reel, a line of the correct weight, a leader, and a fly.

Before leaving home for the lake, stream, or casting pool, make sure to wind the line on the reel and to tuck away one or two spare lines of the same weight in your fishing vest or tackle box. Knot or splice the leader to the tip of the line before leaving home as well. This will save considerable fumbling around and annoyance on your arrival, especially if the air is chilly or the fish are rising.

Upon your arrival at streamside, assemble the fly rod first. Remove the sections from their cloth sack and pull the ferrule plugs from the female ferrules. (Ferrule plugs are normally provided by certain makers of high quality rods. The plugs are inserted into the female ferrules during storage to prevent dirt from entering and scoring the metal when the sections are joined.)

Before joining two sections, lightly lubricate the male ferrule by rotating it against the oily skin at the base of your nose. This removes accumulated dirt and lubricates the ferrule very slightly, which is an aid to joining the sometimes tight-fitting tubes.

If the rod happens to be of ferruleless design, like many of the most popular fiberglass rods are these days, apply a very light coating of hard paraffin to the male joint surface. Paraffin functions as a lubricant on fiberglass and helps one achieve a good tight fit between the sections.

When you're finally ready to mate up the rod sections, grasp them firmly by the ferrules or

reinforced synthetic fiber areas. Make sure the alignment dots or guides are lined up, then push the sections smoothly and firmly together. Guide alignment is especially important on fly rods. The relatively large-diameter fly line won't flow through the guides smoothly if they're badly out of alignment. As a result, long-distance casting will be affected adversely.

Once you've joined all the sections of your rod, attach the reel to the reel seat with the sliding rings or locking mechanism. Make certain the reel is *firmly* attached and doesn't wobble around. Nothing quite matches the irritation of having a reel fall off during a cast while one is standing waist deep in a fast-moving stream, or concentrating on playing a hooked fish.

The next to the last step in assembling the tackle is to thread the fly line through the guides.

All that remains before starting to cast is to tie a fly to the leader tippet with a Return Knot, or any one of several other suitable knots. If you intend to practice your casting at a casting pool, snip the point and barb off the hook.

Fig. 31.   The Return Knot is one of the more reliable fishing knots to tie flies to leader tippets.

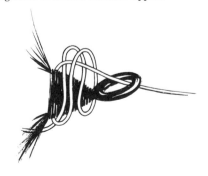

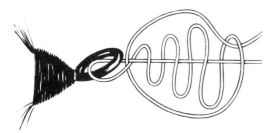

Fig. 32. The Improved Clinch Knot is all right for flies, but far better for lures and plugs.

How to Grip the Rod

No two anglers' hands, forearms, and wrists are precisely the same, nor do they articulate in precisely the same way. As a result, several effective ways for gripping a fly-rod handle have evolved down through the centuries.

The writer prefers to grasp the rod with the thumb resting on top of the handle (or "grip" as it's usually called). See Fig. 33.

This grip has several advantages. For one thing, it helps one maintain a very firm wrist throughout both casting strokes. It is especially suitable for distance casting, because the thumb placed on top of the grip helps apply leverage to the rod.

The grip in which the index finger is extended along the top of the handle, sometimes onto the bamboo or glass butt section itself (Fig. 34), is a good one to use with ultra-light fly rods having abbreviated handles. When casting with relatively short rods like this, the forearm actually serves as an extension of the butt section of the rod and aids in achieving certain specific movements.

Short-range *horizontal* fly-rod strokes are easily made with all the standard methods of holding onto a fly-rod grip, but the "free wrist" grip probably performs these movements most comfortably (Fig. 35). It is accomplished in a fashion similar to shaking hands, except that the wrist is rotated somewhat more—to the right. In the free-wrist grip, the thumb of the casting hand lies along the side of the rod handle.

A variation of the free-wrist grip, in which the first joint of the index finger and the thumb form a sort of pressure ring around the handle (Fig. 36), is also gaining in popularity. Maximum pressure is exerted on those two fingers during the "kick" portions of the casting strokes.

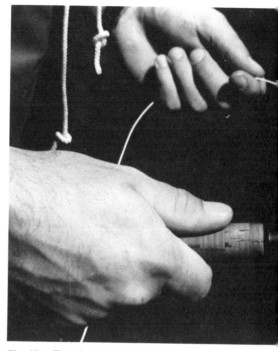

Fig. 33. Thumb on top.

Fig. 34. Extended index finger.

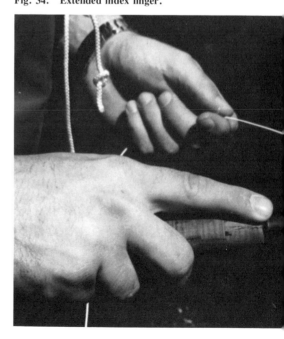

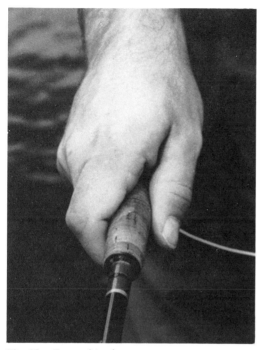

Fig. 35.   Free wrist grip.

Fig. 36.   A variation.

Fig. 37

Stance

Body alignment and balance are also critical factors influencing all types of casting, and especially fly-casting. Most of the casts described in these chapters are most effectively made by assuming a stance in which the left foot is placed slightly in advance of the right (Fig. 37), assuming you are right-handed.

The feet should also be somewhat separated, but never so much as to prevent torso rotation.

At the start of the cast, one's weight should be distributed about evenly between the feet, slightly toward the balls of the feet.

Whether you're casting at poolside, from a boat, or while wading, the basic stance is the same, except when seated or performing a roll cast. In the roll cast the right foot is positioned slightly ahead of the left to permit a quicker-than-normal body turn.

Fly-casting from a seated position in a boat shouldn't be attempted until one has the basic casting strokes well under control.

Fig. 38

Getting the Feel

Learning how to cast with a fly rod is a little easier than learning how to swing a golf club, tennis racquet, or baseball bat. Those items are all relatively stiff and rigid. As a result, one feels little more than their dead weight until contact is made with the ball.

A fly rod, on the other hand, is a lively, flexible, springlike structure with noticeable feel once it's loaded with the weight of a line. How much and how rapidly a rod flexes and unflexes under the influence of that weight defines the feel and timing when the rod is activated by the hand.

In order to get a better idea of what this means, take hold of the rod handle by means of the first of the aforementioned gripping methods (Fig. 33). Assume a stance with your left foot slightly in front of your right, feet spread comfortably apart (Fig. 38).

After working out about 20 feet of fly line, flip the rod tip into a rapidly accelerating up-and-back movement (Fig. 39). Allow the line to flow out behind you until the loop that's formed in it straightens out. Stop the rod tip no farther back than a position approximating one o'clock.

When the line has straightened behind you (Fig. 40), thrust the rod tip forward, abruptly stopping the motion at about ten o'clock (Fig. 41). Before the line falls to the water in front of you, repeat these up-and-back and forward strokes several times, trying to keep the line airborne all the time.

If you're doing it right, you'll *feel* the rod respond to the pulling weight of the line at the end of backward and forward strokes (Fig. 42).

Be sure to hold the line with the fingers of your line hand to prevent it from paying loosely off the reel during the casting movements.

On the next series of exploratory movements,

Fig. 39

Fig. 40

Fig. 41

notice how it's necessary to pause briefly to let the line straighten out in the air behind you. Watch this visually. And this time, before the line has extended itself fully—just as the line loop starts to turn over near the butt section of the leader—start the forward stroke. Experiment with the timing until you can control both directional movements instinctively.

Fig. 42

Basic Overhead Cast

Once you're accustomed to the feel of the rod bending and releasing energy, and the feel of line weight working against the rod, it's time to adjust the movements a bit and try to make some genuine *fishing* casts.

First, line up your torso so that you face 30 to 45 degrees *away* from the direction in which you intend to cast (Fig. 37). This body position permits complete freedom of movement for the arm, shoulder, torso, and elbow. It is crucial to many of the movements to follow.

Begin by holding the rod horizontally, rod tip about a foot from the water in front of you.

The wrist should be firm, cocked slightly downward so the rod extends in a direct line from your forearm (Fig. 43). However, the entire arm should not be extended.

The upper arm should be held out from your side, elbow bent at about a 45-degree angle (Fig. 44). The shoulder, upper arm, and elbow should be relaxed. Grip the rod handle firmly but not tensely. What we'll attempt to do next is *compress* the energy released by the rod by means of shorter rod strokes.

Fig. 43

Fig. 44

Begin the backcast with a progressive squeeze of your casting hand, precisely at the same moment you start lifting the line from the water (Figs. 45 and 46). This squeeze should continue until the tip of the rod reaches its apogee, the twelve-o'clock position. At this instant the grip should be very firm. As you squeeze down during the backcast stroke, notice how the squeezing seems to spring the rod to life, imparting more speed to the tip and thence to the line.

At this point, we should emphasize that the basic overhead backcast stroke consists of a coordinated lifting movement of shoulder, upper arm, lower arm, elbow, wrist, and hand. The wrist should not be intentionally flexed during the backcast lifting stroke. The rod should feel like it is an extension of your forearm.

Depending on the length of your arm, how long a length of line you're lifting from the water, the relative stiffness or limpness of the rod, and the length of the rod itself, your casting hand should travel about 1½ to 2 feet during the backcast stroke.

The direction your hand travels, as viewed from the corner of your right eye, should be upward and only very slightly backward. Stop that movement when your casting hand is about even with your eye . . . and stop it abruptly.

Pause slightly at the top of the backcast to

Fig. 45

Fig. 46

Fig. 47

Fig. 48

allow the line to flow up and back in a loop (Fig. 47).

During the pause, notice the tendency of your wrist to break slightly and let the rod tip drift back to the one- or two-o'clock position. That's OK. Let it happen (Fig. 48). If your backcast has been made with a lift, you can let the rod drift back to a position almost level with the water without unduly influencing the backward flow of line.

The next portion of the cast is essentially a *throwing* movement. For lack of a better analogy, it resembles throwing a baseball, or driving a nail into a wall with a hammer.

The forward casting stroke is a smooth, rapidly accelerating thrust of shoulder, upper arm, elbow, wrist, and hand. It drives the rod tip sharply from the one- or two-o'clock position to about the ten-o'clock position (Fig. 49).

Apply maximum acceleration to the rod between the twelve- and one-o'clock positions (Fig. 50).

Fig. 49
Fig. 50

Fig. 51

Kick

The area of maximum rod-tip acceleration is called the area of the "kick." Kick in fly-casting compares to wrist-snap in baseball or golf. But I must say that it is not truly wrist-snap. Rather, it is that portion of the forward casting stroke during which maximum squeeze is applied to the grip, then terminated with an abrupt little punching motion.

Kick is applied to both the backward and for-ward casting strokes—between eleven and twelve o'clock on the backward movement, and between twelve and ten o'clock on the forward stroke. What makes it come about is your ability to squeeze the grip with control. Kick is the end product of a progressive sort of squeezing that can probably be most closely compared to that used to milk a cow, only harder and timed to achieve its greatest intensity in such a way as to impart a sudden release of energy through the rod tip. See Fig. 51 and Fig. 49.

Casting Plane

If you have snapped the rod into the backcast stroke (Fig. 52) and thrust it forward in the same plane, the line loops have traveled in almost precisely the same vertical path. They have also remained seperated instead of passing one another horizontally in "figure-8" fashion.

On the other hand, if you have tilted your wrist off to one side or the other (Fig. 53), the line may have followed an elliptical path through the air and slapped you on the ear or neck during the forward stroke.

To be sure, a slight separation of the horizontal line plane may not unduly influence your casting at short distances. I can recall hundreds of occasions when slight line-loop separation was needed to deal with specific angling situations, but for the most part, exaggerating loop separation should be avoided. It can really promote bad casting habits in much the same way an improper grip accentuates a sliced or hooked golf shot. So, while you're learning, forget the fancy stuff and develop sound control. Assume elliptical rod-tip movements are anathema for the time being. We'll discuss the specifics of using them effectively in Chapter 11.

Fig. 52

Fig. 53

Chapter 7

Important Refinements

Loop Depth

Whether it's flowing back or forward, the line loop has a depth from top to bottom. The depth of the loop is also known as the "bow" of the line in some regions.

When the loop is a narrow one, say a foot or two, very long straight casts can be made with ease. The comparatively short surface presented to the air by the leading portion of a tight loop encounters less air resistance than a long one.

How one controls the depth of the loop is predicated on a very basic principle of fly-casting. Simply stated, it is that *the line must describe the same path as that described by the rod tip.*

From a practical standpoint, what this means is that if your casting stroke is short and compressed, causing the rod tip to describe a very short arc, the line loop will be relatively narrow. The converse is also true, a wide line loop resulting from a wide casting arc.

To cast a tight line loop, compress your casting strokes into very compact, powerful movements, making certain to snap the rod tip abruptly to a stop at the vertical position at the completion of the backcast. Bring the forward stroke to an abrupt halt at about the eleven-o'clock position (Figs. 54 and 55).

Casting a wide loop takes a lot more finesse. Widening the loop of a cast fly line requires a

Fig. 54. Tight loop.

Fig. 55.   Tight loop, rear view.

Fig. 56.   A properly thrown tight loop straightens the line out well above the surface (below).

Fig. 57

significant widening of the casting arc. And the wider the arc, the more room there is for error.

The principle involved is basic. We mentioned it a moment ago when we said the line must describe the same path as that followed by the rod tip.

First throw a normal high backcast (above).

Impart progressive squeeze, but less kick than in the basic overhead cast. The feel of this cast is one of soft, smooth delicacy (Fig. 57).

As the line flows out behind you, drop your casting hand straight down a few inches, at the same time letting the rod tip drift back to a position between two and three o'clock (Fig. 58).

Fig. 58

Fig. 59

Begin the forward casting stroke (Fig. 59) an instant before the line straightens out. Start with a gentle squeeze of the rod handle. Apply the power slowly and progressively so you feel as if the cast is being made with the middle and butt portion of the rod only.

Complete the forward casting stroke at approx-

imately ten o'clock. However, visually aim the cast at a point in space well over the intended target. Properly executed, the entire fly line and leader will straighten out fully while still in the air. The fly will descent to the water like a feathery puff of thistledown.

Among all the refinements of the basic over-

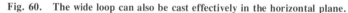

Fig. 60. The wide loop can also be cast effectively in the horizontal plane.

Fig. 61

head cast, casting the wide loop improperly probably results in more chaos than any other fly-rod maneuver. In Fig. 61, observe the wrong way to begin the wide-loop backcast stroke. The angler used insufficient lift and failed to apply power progressively at the outset. Note that the position of the casting hand is only scant inches lower than in the correct method depicted on the preceding pages. The effect on the line is devastating. Note how it falls out of control (Fig. 62), and how the rod shows that casting-hand power was applied too late to lift the line into a rising loop. The angler failed to squeeze the grip at the right time, then overcompensated with arm movement.

As a direct result of the backcast being incorrectly started, the line lacked sufficient velocity to remain airborne. Instead, it slapped noisily into the water behind the caster. Once this had happened, there was no way for the caster to recoup. Instead, he was forced to hurry the start of his forward stroke.

The end result of this casting debacle is that the

Fig. 62

Fig. 63

line will land noisily on the water. The forward loop is indeed a wide one. But the bottom portion of the loop (Fig. 63) is lower in relationship to the surface of the water than it should be at this stage of the forward cast. The line describes an almost elliptical path, instead of one parallel to the bottom of the loop.

Obviously, the middle of the line will strike the water first, before leader turnover. And, in this specific angling situation, a crystalline trout stream, the angler has about as much a chance of enticing a fish into a strike following his series of casting mistakes as he'd have hitting it in the head with a rock at the same distance.

Handling and Shooting Fly Line

"Shooting" lengths of fly line is one of the most important aids to casting. Shooting line means propelling it freely through the guides so as to place the fly in front of a rising fish or extend the cast to reach a distant target.

Shooting line is accomplished in one of several ways and involves a number of ways of handling lengths of line before they're released to flow through the guides. The techniques vary according to how much line is to be shot.

It's rarely necessary to extend a cast more than 10 or 15 feet on a small trout stream. Most of the time, a fellow can wade to an advantageous casting location and eliminate the necessity of reaching out long distances with the fly rod. But when you're fishing lakes or broad streams, then long casting frequently becomes necessary. In those situations the fellow who can't knock out 80 or more feet of fly line really isn't in the game a lot of the time. And here's where learning how to shoot line effectively has its payoff.

Small lengths of line may be gathered in very tight loops and held in the palm of the hand (Figs. 64, 65, and 66). At the completion of the forward casting stroke, the line loops are released to be pulled through the guides by the weight of the cast line.

For extending a cast up to about 15 feet, the line may be held in longer loops in the line hand throughout the basic casting strokes (Figs. 67 and 68), then released as the line loop begins to approach its forward limits. Here again, the *weight* of the moving line pulls the remaining line through the guides.

In the case of making casts from 60 to over 90 feet, holding line coils in the hand becomes impractical. A large number of small hand-held loops tend to catch up on one another when released. Longer loops are also inconvenient to hold and manipulate in the hand. But there are other more satisfactory methods. One is to hold long loops of line between the lips (Fig. 69). Obviously, holding line in the mouth is not recommended when fishing polluted waters.

Another way to control long lengths of line is in a stripping basket (Figs. 70 and 71). The line is gathered into a basket before each new cast is made. No additional manipulations are needed since the line usually flows freely from the basket into the guides. Snarls and tangles are rare. Stripping baskets can be used with regular tapered fly lines or with monofilament shooting lines backing up shooting heads.

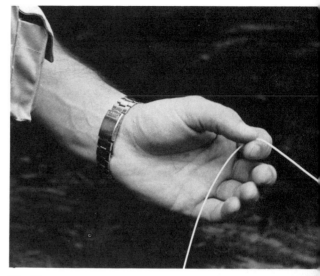

Fig. 64

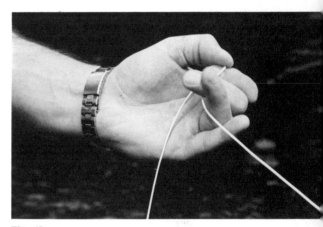

Fig. 65

Fig. 66

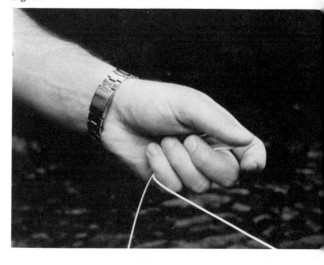

Fig. 67

Fig. 68. Line being "shot."

Fig. 69. Coils of line held by the lips.

Fig. 70

Fig. 71

Fig. 72. "O"-ring shoot.

Add to the above methods the trick of forming an "O" ring with the thumb and index finger of the line hand to direct the line through the butt guide of your fly rod (Fig. 72), and chances are you'll be able to handle virtually any stream situation requiring a sudden extension of casting length. This can add surprisingly to your ability to cover the water efficiently.

Single Line Haul

You may recall how in an earlier chapter we discussed the theoretical aspects of making really long casts with a fly rod. Increased line speed (velocity) was said to be the key factor. Using a very powerful fly rod helps, of course, but that's not always desirable or practical. It's better to increase your own versatility.

Another way to impart additional speed to a fly line is by pulling on it while it's under the influence of rod bend. The technique is discussed here because it relates both to the long-line liftoff to be dealt with later in this chapter, and to the double line haul discussed in Chapter 8.

Right now, we'll consider how to impart more line speed to the backcast stroke.

Make an overhead cast. Make certain that you're casting with at least 30 feet of line. Otherwise, the rod won't be fully loaded with the line weight and the full benefit of increased line velocity won't be realized.

To accomplish the single line haul, pull down very sharply on the line held in your hand during the backcast kick, between eleven and twelve o'clock (Fig. 73).

When attempting to lift a long length of line from the water with the long-line liftoff (discussed on page 83), begin the line haul at the very start of the backcast stroke. This will help break the surface tension between the line and the water.

Complete your cast with a conventional for-

Fig. 73

Fig. 74

ward casting stroke. As you do so, notice how a great deal of additional bend is put in the rod when you pull down on the held line (Figs. 74 and 75). Also notice the effect on the fly line as you release that energy on the next casting stroke.

That feeling is what casters frequently refer to somewhat erroneously as power.

Using the single line haul, casts up to about 60 feet can be made with double-tapered fly lines and light to medium-sized fly rods.

Fig. 75

Fig. 76

Long-Line Liftoff

It's sometimes necessary to quickly lift a long length of line from the water when fishing on lakes, tidal flats, or large streams. The technique combines the single line haul, a very pronounced backcast kick, and a very firm wrist. Don't attempt this maneuver with a sinking fly line; otherwise you may overload your rod and break it.

The trick is to break the surface tension between the line and the water in a fast, progressive, dramatically lifting stroke.

Three things must occur in rapid order. Begin the movement by lifting as much of the extended line from water as possible with the rod (Fig. 76).

Note in Figs. 76 and 77 that Bill Frazer, the caster, is lifting about half of a 60-foot length of line clear of the water, and also beginning to impart a single line haul. Bill, who's sales manager for Scientific Anglers/3M and a very powerful, individualistic caster, incorporates a great deal of wrist break into the backcast following the kick. Other casters use less wrist break and accomplish the drift-back of the rod tip with more arm extension. Precisely how this is done is irrelevant, really, and depends mostly on style rather than basic technique. The main thing is to start the line moving up and back very firmly through the kick and release of energy.

Fig. 77

Fig. 78

Properly made, the line will remain airborne throughout the backcast (Fig. 78). The forward casting stroke will be started as the line loop begins to straighten out (Fig. 79).

Skip ahead to Fig. 80 and notice that Bill has imparted an additional movement to the line hand into the forward stroke. It is a second sharp pull on the line, and its function is to add even greater speed to the line. It will be described in the section on the double line haul in the next chapter.

Fig. 81 illustrates what takes place when insufficient lift is imparted to the backcast during the long-line liftoff.

Fig. 79

Fig. 80.   Forward stroke includes a second line haul.

Fig. 81.   Insufficient lift results in this sort of disaster.

Fig. 82

Roll-Cast Liftoff

For fishing small streams and where great delicacy of presentation is needed, the counterpart of the long-line liftoff is the roll-cast liftoff. It permits lifting up to about 50 feet of line from the water with a minimum of surface disturbance and is one of the basic tools of the dry-fly and nymph angler on smooth-surfaced lakes and streams.

Start the roll-cast liftoff by lifting the rod tip smoothly and slowly to a vertical position (Fig. 82).

Fig. 83

Drive the rod tip forward smartly to the ten-o'clock position (Fig. 83).

This causes the line to literally "roll" forward and lift from the water (Fig. 84).

Fig. 84

Fig. 85

Before the line has a chance to fall back onto the surface, snatch it up into a conventional back-cast (Fig. 85), and complete your presentation with false casts and a delivery stroke (Fig. 86).

Fig. 86

Chapter 8

Distance Fly-Casting

How far one casts with a fly rod is relative to several variable factors: the casting tackle, the skill of the caster, and the climatic conditions of the moment. Before we consider them individually, however, we should really define what we mean by "distance."

Casts that would be considered quite long for an ultra-light fly rod most certainly would fall far short of the booming 200-footers attainable with powerful tournament rods. A distant rising fish or target ring that might confound the tyro, on the other hand, could be a moderate distance for one of consummate casting skill and experience. Headwinds might shorten the beginner's casting potential by as much as 50 percent, where the advanced caster might experience only a slight reduction in attainable distance. So when we speak of distance casting, we're really talking about the ability to get the most out of our tackle, cast to the limit of our acquired skill, and minimize those external forces, such as wind and gravity, that further limit our capabilities and those of the tackle.

Although the angling caster is not always forced to test his tackle and technique to the utmost, learning how to make long casts does have some genuine benefits. It results not only in extending the fishing radius, but also in improving overall line and line-loop control, which increases casting effectiveness at the shorter distances as well. However, these benefits are not always clearly or immediately manifest to the tyro. Their importance does not become fully evident until one has cast seriously for a considerable length of time and in a wide range of situations.

The distance caster needs to understand his tackle, have good coordination, and master the various special techniques that add distance.

Tackle

Let's start with the assumption that every fly rod has defined limits to those qualities which enable it to function effectively. Each rod can be loaded with only so much energy. Only so much energy can be released. A given rod can do only so much work . . . no more.

Short, light-action fly rods simply cannot cast as far as long, powerful rods. A 75-foot cast with a 5½-foot ultra-light midge rod is truly splendid, while a cast of the same distance is a moderate one for a 9½-foot heavy-duty steelhead rod equipped with a 10-weight shooting head. The latter outfit is capable of casting well in excess of 100 feet under angling conditions. So, it's quite important to put distance in perspective when we start talking about long-range casting. Distance is relative to many things. Tackle is only one of them.

The Caster

Some individuals never become good casters, mostly because they're unwilling to work at it. Others, perhaps with considerably less raw talent, become capable casters as a direct result of hard work and diligent practice.

Probably the majority of angler/casters fall into the former category. They have neither the time nor the burning desire to become the world's greatest fisherman nor the next North American amateur distance champion. And as I said a moment ago, the value of distance casting doesn't always make itself obvious to one seeking a level of somewhat less than perfection itself. The mental side of casting tends to cause some learners to

Fig. 87.   Big water—long casts.

Fig. 88

halt prematurely in their efforts to become better casters—to become discouraged by the practice and hard work it takes before results begin to show at the end of the rod.

Another human factor is more physical. Some persons are stronger and have better timing than others. Some are utterly incapable of becoming casting masters because of an inbred lack of coordination, poor eyesight, or other physical handicaps. The best they can hope for, like handicapped golfers, is to overcome those handicaps to the best of their ability. The more intense the desire, usually, the better the results.

And let's face some angling realities. Once the fly-casting distance exceeds 80 feet, the chances of hooking fish decrease dramatically. So for the nontournament caster, there truly is a point of diminishing return when casting for distance.

Certain basic techniques are universal to both fishing and tournament casting. They are the double line haul and precise loop control.

Double Line Haul

This technique goes one step farther than the single line haul described in the last chapter. It imparts additional line speed to the cast during both the backward and the forward casting strokes.

Double-hauling is accomplished by means of four distinct line-hand movements. These are imparted in concert with the regular rod strokes.

The first phase of the double line haul is exactly the same as the single line haul. As the rod enters the kick area on the backward stroke, pull down sharply on the held line (Fig. 88). Grasp the line below the stripping guide in order to get a longer haul. If more than about 30 feet of line is to be lifted from the water, start the first haul simultaneously with the rod lift during the initial backcast in order to help break the surface tension with the water.

Allow your line hand to drift up to the stripping

Fig. 89

guide as the line loop courses back and up (Fig. 89). If you need to lengthen the casting portion of the line to more adequately load the rod action, release line as the backcast flows out. If even more line is needed, release it on the forward stroke too.

Fig. 90

Begin the forward stroke with the rod only (Fig. 90).

Fig. 91

As you thrust forward into the kick (Fig. 91), make a similar downward haul on the line.

Fig. 92

Shoot and release the held line (Fig. 92), as described in the previous chapter.

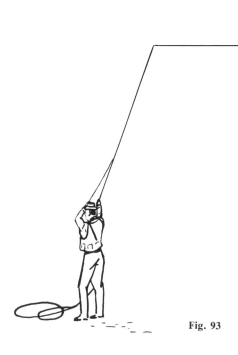

Loop Control

Loop control and configuration are ultracritical in distance fly-casting. If the loop is very tight and configured in a perfectly vertical plane, maximum distance can be expected from the cast (Fig. 93).

In practice, this means that one makes false casts until the backward loop is satisfactorily configured before making the final delivery. Two or three false casts are usually sufficient to achieve the right loop shape and alignment.

Fig. 93

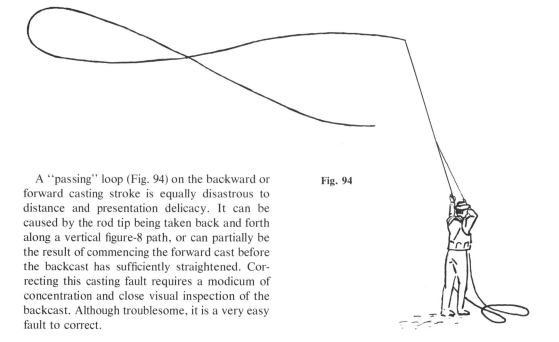

Fig. 94

A "passing" loop (Fig. 94) on the backward or forward casting stroke is equally disastrous to distance and presentation delicacy. It can be caused by the rod tip being taken back and forth along a vertical figure-8 path, or can partially be the result of commencing the forward cast before the backcast has sufficiently straightened. Correcting this casting fault requires a modicum of concentration and close visual inspection of the backcast. Although troublesome, it is a very easy fault to correct.

Some Additional Errors

Grip and squeeze errors can also contribute to ineffective distance casting. And probably the most noteworthy of these mistakes is canting the rod off the vertical plane (Fig. 95). This is common even among some of the most proficient and expert casters. It is also very difficult for the caster himself to detect. An inch of vertical tilt at the hand, resulting from improper squeeze or wrist/arm position at the start of a cast, may result in many inches of error at the rod tip, depending on the length of the rod.

Fig. 95. Rod viewed from front.

Fig. 96. Lake fly-fishing demands distance, accuracy, and loop control.

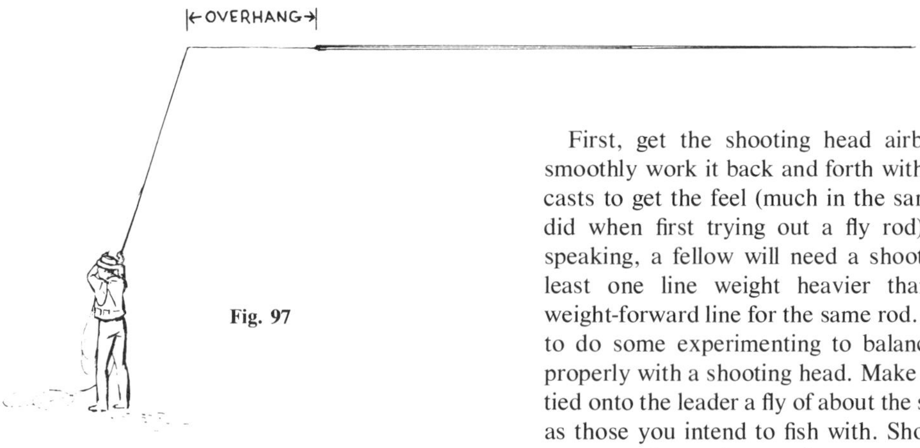

|←OVERHANG→|

Fig. 97

Casting the Shooting Head

Shooting-head fly lines backed with either mono-filament nylon or braided nylon shooting line are cast very much like conventional weight-forward lines—with a small difference.

When casting a shooting head, a length of shooting line must be allowed between the butt of the shooting head and the rod tip to prevent the spliced loop from striking the rod tip. This allowed space between the "head" and the rod tip is called "overhang" (Fig. 97).

About 4 to 6 feet of overhang is usually sufficient for fishing casts. However, when one makes the exaggerated line-hauling movements of tournament distance casting, more separation is needed. Precisely how much depends not only on the length of the pull, but also on the critical rod/line balance and the placement of the stripping guide on the rod's butt section.

Once you have noted the length of overhang that lets you get the most out of a given rod/line combination, mark the shooting line with indelible dye at the point where your line hand will grasp it during the haul.

There are some other small differences between casting a shooting head and a conventional line as well. For one thing, the shooting-head line (being a single-taper instead of a weight-forward design) behaves somewhat differently than the latter once airborne. Probably the best advice I can give is to accentuate smoothness throughout the entire group of casting movements.

First, get the shooting head airborne. Then smoothly work it back and forth with a few false casts to get the feel (much in the same way you did when first trying out a fly rod). Generally speaking, a fellow will need a shooting head at least one line weight heavier than a proper weight-forward line for the same rod. You'll have to do some experimenting to balance your rod properly with a shooting head. Make sure you've tied onto the leader a fly of about the same weight as those you intend to fish with. Shooting heads are normally used most often to cast fairly heavy steelhead, salmon, and saltwater flies. Many such flies are relatively air-resistant. As a result a somewhat heavier line may be required to achieve appropriate velocities.

Avoid overshocking the rod tip during the forward kick. Load the rod with line weight, then release that stored energy in as smooth a delivery as possible.

Fig. 98. **Shooting heads pay off!**

Chapter 9

Fly Casts in the Overhead Plane

Changing Direction

You've been running nymphs next to the deeply undercut, grassy banks for a couple of hours. It's a lazily warm spring day, the fish aren't biting, and your casting and retrieving has settled down into a steady, unthinking, monotonous rhythm. You pick the line from the water for another cast quartering across and downstream. The loop of amber-colored line flows up and back smoothly, neatly bisecting a narrow gap between two hemlock branches. You edge downstream a few feet while false-casting, not quite so sure that you could drop the loop between those branches for a second time.

As you accelerate the tip of your little split-cane rod into a forward cast delivery, a flitting cardinal catches your eye, then suddenly in the black-gold currents beneath it, a flash of bronze makes your heart skip.

What do you do now? You're too close to the right-hand bank to make a backcast in that direction. If you wait until wading to a more opportune position downstream, the fish may be off-station.

What do you do next? The forward cast is nearing its completion. In a moment, you may have lost the opportunity to work on one of the few fish you've spotted feeding all day.

As the line courses on toward the initial target, you pivot your torso to the left. The loop begins to straighten. You drive the slender cane shaft in the new direction, slightly upstream from where the trout disclosed his feeding position. The line, like an obedient pet on a leash, follows the new path described by the rod tip. The fly drops into the current inches from the bank, settling deeply in seconds.

There's a flash—a heavy tug! And after several anxious minutes of trying to keep the powerful 22-incher from entangling your line in a submerged snag, it's gratefully brought to net and released unharmed.

Sudden changes in casting direction are among the most common maneuvers required of the fly-caster. The need for directional changes arises not only on streams, but as in the case of our imaginary anecdote, also when fishing lakes or tidal flats where fish activity is frequently observed in directions opposed to those of one's casting strokes.

The directional change is one of the simplest casting maneuvers in the vertical plane. Observe the angler in Fig. 99. He has almost completed the delivery strokes.

As in the anecdote, he has spotted a fish feeding under the bushes shading the opposite bank. So in Fig. 100 you see him start the body pivot as the line begins to straighten on the forward stroke. The caster drives the cast in the new direction (Fig. 101).

Fig. 102 shows that the directional change was most successful.

Another type of directional change might have come about from this situation. Had the fish been located more downstream than it was, the caster would have had to pivot and deliver the directional change on a backcast stroke instead.

Casting in the Wind

Of the natural forces and hazards influencing one's casting, wind is the most difficult to deal with in terms of its force, direction, and unpredictability. However, it is possible to modify one's casting techniques to deal with many of the

Fig. 99.   Cast is begun in downstream direction.

Fig. 100.   Body pivot begins as line starts to straighten.

Fig. 101.   The rod is stroked in a new direction.

Fig. 102.   Result: a beautiful presentation under the bushes.

Fig. 103.   Blustery weather gives good fishing—tough casting.

probable variances of wind. Some of the modifications can be best accomplished in the vertical casting plane, others in the horizontal. A few, like winds blowing at gale force and harder, normally necessitate a complete halt to one's casting efforts with fly-fishing tackle.

Tailwind

Tailwinds blowing up to about 15 knots are the easiest winds to cope with. The main thing to remember when casting in a following wind is to impart enough kick to the backcast stroke to straighten the line out against the moving air. Stronger tailwinds usually make casting an impossibility. However, they don't always call a total halt to the fishing. I recall fishing in situations where the wind was blowing so hard one could flip the line vertically into the air and the force of the wind would carry it out far enough to permit fishing out the cast.

To be sure, that kind of situation doesn't promote pleasant fishing or rhythmic casting, but fish can be caught on flies under those conditions. And after all, the true test of the caster is how well he copes with the conditions of the moment, no matter how adverse they may be.

Fig. 104

Headwind

Headwinds up to about 15 knots are also fairly easy to deal with, provided, of course, the caster has good loop control and a grasp of the single and double line haul. When casting in the vertical rod plane, moderate headwinds shouldn't affect one's ability to make a presentation to moderate distances much one way or the other. The trick is to let the wind do some of the work.

In Fig. 104, I have made a normal high back-cast, but on the forward stroke imparted a powerful single line haul and driven the rod tip down very sharply toward the water. If the forward stroke is firm enough, the line will flow just above the surface in an extremely tight loop. The wind will keep the line from striking the water short of the target. You can see this happening in the illustration. Note the rod flexed strongly almost to the water.

Fig. 105

Fig. 105 shows the line lifted by the wind as predicted. The loop was very tight and almost V-shaped.

The small surface presented to the wind by the tight loop sliced through the air like a knife (Fig. 106). Weight-forward lines are recommended.

Fig. 106

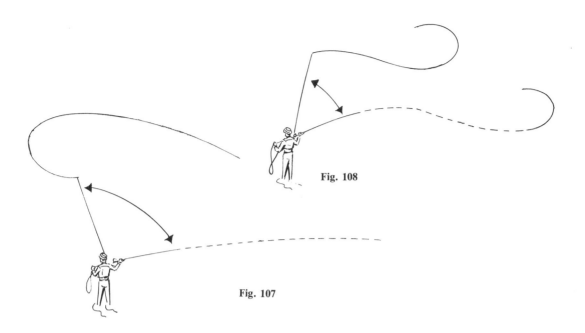

Fig. 108

Fig. 107

Crosswind

Winds addressing the caster from either side can be handled with casting adaptations in both vertical and horizontal casting planes. Surprisingly, the longest casts can be made most effectively (and safely) utilizing the vertical plane.

One method of dealing with crosswind is to cast a very tight loop with a long, stiff, quick rod. For the polished caster, this is perhaps the most satisfactory method. But for the beginner or one casting a shooting head (which tends to drift badly in a crosswind), an easier technique is to literally *roll* the line out in such a way that the fly is always positioned higher than the caster's head.

Here's how it's done. Deliver the backcast stroke with great firmness and a powerful squeeze to the one-o'clock position. Allow the rod tip to drift back to a position almost horizontal to the water behind you (Fig. 107). Deliver the forward casting stroke slowly and progressively, using the middle and butt sections of the rod only (Fig. 108). Impart a final little kick to provide leader turnover. Properly done, the line rolls forward in a very wide, exaggerated loop, the fly always well above the head (Fig. 109). It's a technique that requires a lot of practice to really master, but once learned, permits safe casting for distances up to 80 feet in stiff crosswinds and when using lead-head lines. Practice to learn the method should always be done *in a crosswind* and using a

piece of yarn knotted to the tippet instead of a practice fly.

Fairly short crosswind casts are most easily accomplished by the backhand cast described in the next chapter.

Fig. 109

Fig. 110

Slack-Line Casts

Varying speeds of current between the caster and his target area pull on the line and cause the fly to race unnaturally past or over the fish. The drag conditions can be counteracted to varying degrees by causing the line and leader to drop slackly to the surface, or by "mending" the cast in an upstream or downstream direction, depending on the placement of the various speeds of current between the caster and the fish. Mending takes the tension out of the line.

Long-Tippet Technique

This technique of Bill Lawrence's permits the caster to compress 8 to 15 feet of fine leader tippet upon itself, achieving a perfect float of a dry fly in currents of widely varying speeds.

The following illustrations (Figs. 111, 112, and 113) show three classic situations in which conventional slack-line casts most probably would fail to elicit strikes from larger trout.

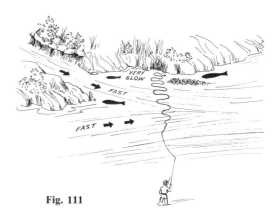

Fig. 111

The first (Fig. 111) is a situation on a limestone stream in which a 3-pound brown trout was coaxed into taking. The weedy island was about 4 feet long. The channel between the island and the bank was about 8 inches wide. The fish in the "V" between the bank and the fast current is somewhat easier to get at. But it would still take the long-tippet technique to achieve a long enough float to provide the fish an adequate look-see at the artificial.

The second situation (Fig. 112) is common on meadow water. The fly must be floated down a narrow channel. Such a float is difficult, because, just as the fly approaches the fish, the tippet may catch on weeds, creating drag. Then, down goes the fish.

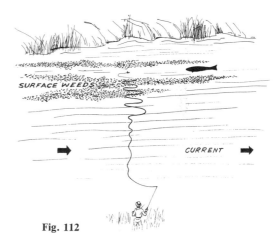

Fig. 112

In the third situation (Fig. 113), the current is extremely bubbly and turbulent next to the bank. To complicate matters, it's almost impossible for the angler to see the fly. Frequently, a fish in a place like this rises so quietly it may not be seen.

The rod needed to make really effective long-tippet casts is a specialized tool. And, in the modern vernacular, the leader itself is "out of sight."

According to Milt Kahl of the Pasadena Casting Club, who cast for the photos to follow, the best rod for long-tippet casting on small to medium-sized streams is a 7-footer with a soft tip. This is matched with a 5-weight double-tapered floating fly line.

For a leader, Milt recommends a 9-foot knotless leader tapered from .017 to .006 or .005. To this is tied a 15-foot-long tippet of .006 or .005 monofilament. This is just right for flies up to size 16. Longer tippets aren't recommended. Tippets longer than 15 feet are difficult to deliver with authority in the wind.

For larger streams an 8-foot rod with a 7-weight double-tapered line, a 9-foot leader tapering from .022 to .010, and 15 feet of .010 tippet would be about right.

Leader butt size is critical. The terminal tackle used on a 5-weight line can't be used with a 7-weight line.

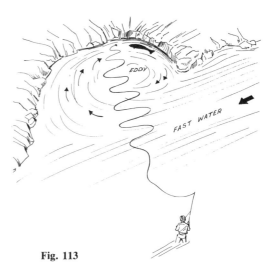

Fig. 113

The beginner should probably start with 8 feet of tippet, then lengthen it out as he becomes more proficient.

In the remarkable photo sequence to follow we'll pick up the cast at the top of the backward stroke. Note the extreme *compression* of the forward stroke in Figs. 114 and 115. The effect of the forward wrist snap may be seen in Figs. 116 and 117. Figs. 118 and 119 illustrate the wavy configuration that's intentionally put into the line with the soft rod tip, which when transmitted on to the leader, causes it to *pile up* in a series of tight loops (Fig. 120), creating the needed slack for a drag-free float. Fig. 121 shows rod action rendered from ultra-high-speed photos.

Fig. 114. The long-tippet technique rod stroke is compressed and . . .

Fig. 115. . . . culminates with abrupt wrist-snap.

Fig. 116.   Effect of wrist-snap begins to show here . . .

Fig. 117.   . . . becoming more pronounced as energy is released.

Fig. 118.   The line follows the path described by the rod tip and . . .

Fig. 119.   . . . forms into a wavy configuration which . . .

Fig. 120.   . . . causes the tippet to "pile" upon itself.

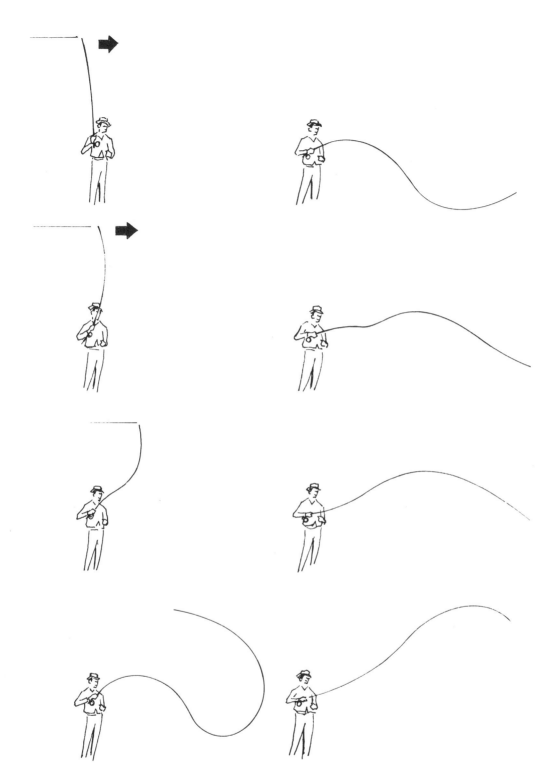

Fig. 121. Long-tippet technique—forward stroke and wrist-snap.

Fig. 122. Slack-line casts help fool larger trout like this fine rainbow.

Fig. 123

Lazy-S Cast

The lazy-S cast is normally employed when a very short drag-free float is needed. The author prefers to use this cast when fishing slow-moving water and only when fishing across current of uniform speed against an undercut bank, over a channel between weeds, against a rock cliff, or in some similar situation.

The technique is ridiculously simple. Make a backcast in the vertical plane. Then, at the completion of the forward stroke and before the loop has quite straightened, waggle the rod tip back and forth very vigorously a few times (Fig. 123).

Check Cast

The check cast accomplishes about the same end result as the lazy-S cast. It can be performed in both vertical and horizontal casting planes. Current speed should be uniform between the caster and his target. Normal backcast and forward casting strokes are made (Fig. 124).

As the line begins to turn over and straighten from the forward loop, the rod tip is given a noticeable vertical jerk (Fig. 125). This causes the line to drop loosely onto the surface (Fig. 126).

Fig. 127 shows the line configuration imparted by the check cast from a higher angle. It coincides in sequence with Fig. 126.

Fig. 124

Fig. 125. As the loop turns over, the rod tip is given a short jerk.

Fig. 126.   The line falls in loose curves to the surface . . .

Fig. 127.   . . . permitting a short drag-free drift.

Fig. 128.   High banks and overhanging bushes call for roll-casting.

Fig. 129

Roll Cast

Roll-casting permits one to deliver a fly in situations when no backcast is possible, such as in narrow, tunnel-like brush and tree-lined stretches of streams and along high banks.

Although the roll cast can be performed in several ways, one of the easiest is to start by raising the rod tip in a moderate, progressive lift to the vertical position (Fig. 129), taking care not to break all the surface tension between the line and the water.

Do not use weight-forward lines for roll-casting. They won't turn over properly at the completion of the cast. If you will be fishing where long casts are needed, in addition to roll casts, then use one of the new long-belly weight-forward lines, the front ends of which perform like double-tapered lines.

Position the right foot slightly in advance of the

Fig. 130

Fig. 131

left for the most effective roll-cast presentation. Deliver the forward stroke to a point well over the target. Watch the line literally roll off the water and straighten out in the air in front of you (Figs. 130 and 131).

Properly executed, the roll cast can be used to extend line up to about 50 feet. Any line you want to shoot should be coiled in medium-sized loops in your line hand at the start of the cast. When the rod is about halfway through the forward stroke,

swing your line hand forward toward the butt guide and release a little line. Continue roll-casting until the line is extended to the required distance.

Don't count on spectacular results at the start. Really effective roll-casting requires a lot of practice to learn the precise point at which to release the line for the shoot and the amount of thrust needed to lift the rolling line completely free of the water.

Fig. 132

Snatch Roll Cast

Roll-casting tends to drag a fly through the surface film of the water. This, in turn, drowns a dry fly in short order, waterlogging it so quickly that only a few good floats can be made without changing flies.

The snatch roll cast prevents having to make frequent changes of dry flies in roll-casting situations.

Start by grasping the leader a foot or two from the fly with the line hand (Fig. 132). Make the backward lift of the rod, just as in the conventional roll cast.

Fig. 133

If it's necessary to extend some line, work out the needed length by making roll casts but without releasing your grip on the leader (Fig. 133).

Fig. 134

Once the line has been extended half the distance to the target by means of the false roll casts, make the final delivery stroke (Fig. 134).

Fig. 135

Release your grip on the leader precisely when you would normally shoot the line, allowing the line to roll out to the target area (Fig. 135).

Fig. 136

Pendulum Cast

This very soft cast permits the angler to cast under overhanging bushes without resorting to horizontal (sidearm) casting strokes. Instead of employing the conventional rod stroke in which kick is imparted, in Fig. 136 I sweep the line off the water with the rod in a vertical position. By keeping the rod hand low, I am able to "swing" the tip back and forth, imparting enough momentum to the double-tapered line to form a horizontally configured loop (Fig. 137)—which cozies the fly very gently under the overhanging bushes. Hardly a distance cast—but very handy.

Fig. 137

Fig. 138

Tower Cast

Quite a large number of streamside and lakeside impediments, including high banks, streamside brush, and trees, necessitate higher than normal backcasts.

Of the several ways to effect a high, climbing backcast, perhaps the most dramatically accentuated one is called the tower or steeple cast.

It is begun with the rod tip held as close as possible to the water. The backward stroke (Fig. 138) is made with a swift, vertical sweep of the rod tip to the eleven-o'clock position, but instead of stopping the arm there, as in the pause of a normal backcast, continue lifting until your arm is fully extended overhead (Fig. 139).

Before the line loop completely unfurls, drop your casting hand to shoulder level, elbow bent, and direct the forward stroke somewhat higher than normal, accentuating the follow-through. The cast isn't practical at distances much more than 50 feet or when wading very deeply.

Fig. 139

Fig. 140

Surface-Tension Loading

Occasionally when roll-casting, one needs to make a cast to a rise almost straight upstream. And although the following exercise may risk overloading the rod, the trout at the other end may be worth the gamble.

Stressing a rod with the resistance of surface tension is definitely not a trick to be attempted by the tyro caster, nor with one's most treasured and ancient split-cane rod.

Smoothness of movement and lift must be accentuated. If the line has drifted downstream and is hanging in the current, as it usually is (Fig. 140), the rod is swept up with a smooth lifting stroke that's rather slow in tempo (Figs. 141 and 142) until about half the line is off the water. You'll *feel* the rod load with line weight at a certain point, and that's where to impart a little kick into the stroke (Fig. 143). Correctly done, the line will completely clear the water, flow out, and go on its way to completion.

Fig. 141

Fig. 142.   Sweep the rod with a smooth, lifting stroke . . .

Fig. 143.   . . . and when it loads, impart the kick.

Chapter 10

Fly Casts in the Horizontal Plane

Basic Horizontal Cast

Fly line can be cast with the rod stroked in any plane from vertical to parallel with the water. The secrets of effective casting in horizontal planes are very much the same as for the vertical casts— the backward and forward strokes should describe nearly the same plane back and forth. Excessive plane separation causes many of the major casting problems beginners encounter.

Viewed from above and to the front, the basic horizontal cast is easy to visualize. Make the backcast with a slightly up and back stroke (Fig. 144).

Fig. 144

Deliver the forward cast in the same plane (Fig. 145), taking care not to drop the rod tip at either end of the strokes. This requires a very firm wrist. False casts and the delivery should be firm but delicate.

Since few angling situations require the use of a perfectly flat horizontal delivery, an arc somewhere between vertical and horizontal will usually suffice. Figs. 146 and 147 show a water-level view of the basic cast in a semi-horizontal plane.

Fig. 145

Fig. 146

Fig. 147

Backhand Cast

One of the most useful of all the casts delivered in horizontal or semi-horizontal planes is the backhand cast. Backhanded casting simply means casting over your opposing shoulder. And it's a great way to counter light crosswinds and streamside bushes, and to throw negative (right-hand) curve casts.

The strokes are delivered diagonally across the chest at any desired angle between near-vertical and fully horizontal. Figs. 148 and 149 illustrate the basic strokes delivered in a crosswind.

Figs. 150 and 151 show backhand casting in an almost flat, horizontal plane with the angler attempting a delivery under an overhanging branch.

Backhanded casting is pretty much restricted to distances under 50 feet. You need superior timing and a lot of wrist development in order to perform this cast with accuracy.

Fig. 148

Fig. 149

Fig. 150

Fig. 151

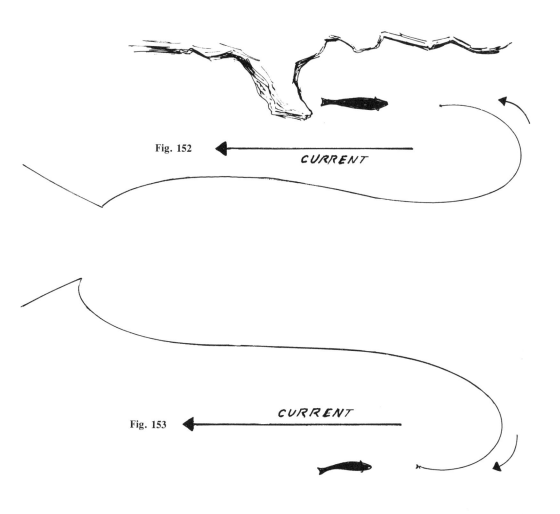

Fig. 152 ←——————— CURRENT

Fig. 153 ←——————— CURRENT

Curve Casts

Casts curving to the left or right of the caster are normally made to present the fly to the fish in advance of the leader tippet, or to deliver it on the far side of some obstruction like a rock or snag.

When a cast is made to curve to the right of a right-handed caster it is referred to as a *negative* curve cast. One bending to the left is a *positive* curve cast (see Figs. 152 and 153).

Negative curve casts are most easily made with the backhand cast just described. Use a double-tapered line and a straight-tapered leader for the negative curve.

To make the cast, take the rod back diagonally across your opposing shoulder. Deliver the forward stroke with a decided kick and an abrupt checking movement to the rod tip (Figs. 154 and 155).

The positive curve cast is easier. Make the rod strokes in a horizontal plane (Fig. 156). Use a double-tapered line and a tapered weight-forward leader for the positive curve. Check the rod sharply at the completion of the forward stroke (Fig. 157).

The degree of curve will depend on how sharply you check the forward stroke and how much kick you put into the delivery (Fig. 158). A headwind will also affect how abruptly the line bends around into a curved shape.

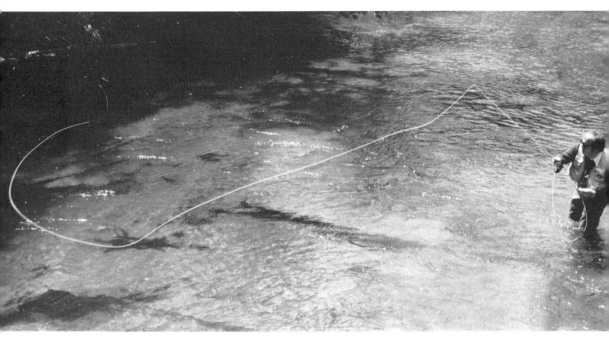

Fig. 154.   Negative curve cast is begun with a backhanded backstroke. Forward cast is delivered with authority.

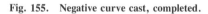

Fig. 155.   Negative curve cast, completed.

Fig. 156.   Positive curve cast. Make a horizontal delivery with great authority . . .

Fig. 157.   . . . then check forward stroke abruptly to snap line into the curve.

Fig. 158.   Result: a perfectly executed curve cast.

Fig. 159

Bow-and-Arrow Cast

One of the less frequently used casts made in the horizontal plane, the bow-and-arrow cast comes into play mostly when fishing very heavily brush-lined small streams where backcasts are impossible and roll casts would result in the fly becoming entangled.

To make a bow-and-arrow cast, grasp the butt section of the leader near the splice with the line (Fig. 159). Pull back on it far enough to put a pronounced bend into your fly rod. Release the held line. It will whip around and extend quite rapidly. The maneuver is restricted to short casts up to about 15 feet. Be careful not to hook your hand or clothing.

Chapter 11

Fly Casts with Elliptical Movements

Elliptical Cast

Perhaps you'll recall how in Chapter 6, explaining the basic overhead cast, we pointed out that widely separating the loop planes tends to promote some troublesome casting habits.

There are some angling situations, however, in which intentional loop-plane separation solves certain difficulties. Virtually all of them flow from the need for a continually rising backcast, such as when backcasting well over the grass and weeds on a high stream bank or into a restricted gap between tree branches.

The rest of the time, elliptical rod strokes tend to be self-defeating in terms of both accuracy and distance, although some authorities may contest the point.

The basic elliptical cast is far easier to learn than the conventional overhead cast in that there is no pause at the top of the backward stroke. All the movements in the elliptical cast flow one from the other in a continuous sequence.

The following sequence of front and side views shows that the backcast stroke is begun in the horizontal plane with a sweeping movement of the rod (Fig. 160).

Fig. 160

Fig. 161

Fig. 161 shows the line flowing up and back in a climbing, horizontal loop.

The loop continues to rise all the way to the outer limit of the backcast stroke (Fig. 162).

Fig. 162

Fig. 163

The forward stroke flows directly from the backcast without hesitation (Fig. 163), and is made with a motion approximating the throwing of a baseball. Note that the loop is in perfect alignment.

Fig. 164

Belgian Backcast

The Belgian backcast achieves the same effect as the elliptical cast, i.e. a constantly climbing back-cast loop. However, unlike the elliptical cast, it is one of the most difficult of the rod strokes to really master.

The backcast stroke is begun much the same as in the elliptical cast, with a semi-horizontal sweep of the rod. However, that's where the similarity ends, because to the sweeping stroke is added a very pronounced outward rotation of the wrist. As the rod reaches the top of the upward movement, the rotating wrist imparts a sharp kick to the rod tip. Figs. 164 and 165 illustrate the effect of the rotating wrist and kick.

Fig. 165

Fly Casts with Elliptical Movements

Chapter 12

Casting with Spinning Tackle

Assembling the Tackle

Care in assembling the tackle is no less important with spinning, spin-casting, and bait-casting equipment than it is with fly rods, reels, and lines. The elements to be assembled are the rod, the spinning reel, a spool of line, and the lure, bait, or practice plug.

Join the rod sections precisely as you would a fly rod. Unless your spinning rod is made from split cane, chances are it will be made in one of the various popular ferruleless designs. If not, then prepare the ferrules as you would a fly rod's, lightly lubricating the male joint on the oily skin at the side of the nose.

One of the keys to effective casting with spinning tackle is the care and preparation of the reel itself—how much care is taken to ensure that it is well lubricated and running smoothly, and whether or not the spool is properly filled with line.

Probably the most common fault found on a tyro's spinning equipment is a spool that's been either overfilled or underfilled with monofilament. Too much line on the reel results in coils of line springing off the spool during the cast, then becoming tangled when the lure is sped on its way.

An underfilled spool results in the line not paying out smoothly, reducing to varying degrees the distance attainable with the cast.

The spool should be filled precisely to where the flange starts to curve—absolutely no farther and very little less. When the line becomes shortened as a result of clipping off worn end lengths, change it for a new one. Even the best monofilament is relatively inexpensive. And it is pointless to cripple one's casting just to save a few pennies. The most economical way to purchase spinning

line is on ¼-pound spools, containing hundreds of yards of line.

Spinning line should be spooled evenly and in very close coils. The best way to do this is on a line-winding machine. A lot of fellows build their own out of small electric motors to which are wired rheostats to control the winding speed. When the spool is properly filled with line, slip a medium-wide flat knotted rubber band over the filled portion of the spool. This will keep the line from unwinding when it's not in use. The knot on the rubber band is tied there to simplify grasping the band for removal.

If the spinning rod is made in more than one section, then care should also be taken in aligning the guides. Spinning-rod guide alignment isn't as critical as it is with fly rods, but casting distance will be affected if they're badly out of alignment.

Some spinning rods are made without locking reel seats. These are the kinds with simple knurled rings that slide over the reel foot to hold the reel firmly against the cork rings of the grip. On this type of grip, make sure the rings are pushed as close to the reel's stem as possible to prevent the reel from loosening and falling off during a cast or when a fish is being played.

How to Grip the Spinning Rod

Spinning rods are grasped similarly to the way fly rods are—with the thumb-on-top grip (Fig. 166). Let the stem of the reel slide naturally between the middle finger and the ring finger.

This allows one to easily drop the index finger (Fig. 167) to lift the line from the pickup friction guide or roller.

Fig. 166

Fig. 167

Fig. 168

Fig. 169

Ready the reel for casting by lifting the line from the pickup roller with the tip of the index finger (Fig. 168).

Swing the bail open until it locks (Figs. 169 and 170). Once the bail is locked open, you're ready to begin casting.

Fig. 170

Fig. 171.   The author lands a 3-pound shad—a great fish on spinning tackle.

Fig. 172

Basic Overhead Spinning Cast

This most fundamental of spinning casts for fishing is made mostly with wrist-snap. For short and moderate casts where accuracy may be important, the upper arm should be held quite close to the body throughout the casting strokes to bring the rod tip into alignment with your eye.

Begin by aiming the rod tip to a point well over the target. Lift the line from its roller guide and open the bail.

Begin the backcast stroke by dipping the rod tip a few inches (Fig. 172). Snap the rod briskly back to the twelve-o'clock position (Figs. 173 and 174).

The movement is a wrist snap combined with a

Fig. 173

Fig. 174

Fig. 175

Fig. 176

slight forearm lift. The hand moves less than a foot in either direction.

If your rod has a classic spinning action—slow and parabolic—then you may need to pause very slightly at the top of the backcast stroke for the rod action to load with casting weight (Fig. 175).

Once the rod loads with casting weight, briskly snap the tip forward to about ten o'clock, imparting a pronounced kick (Fig. 176).

Release the line held by the index finger at the completion of the stroke. Some casters touch the line with the finger to control distance.

Fig. 177

Fig. 178

Soft-Bait Cast

Sometimes the fragile quality of the bait being cast necessitates a swung or lobbed cast, rather than one snapped out with a brisk wrist movement.

A lobbed cast can be made in any rod plane from vertical to fully horizontal. However, before describing the technique, let me offer a word of caution. If you're casting from a boat containing other anglers, or from the bank of a lake or stream where other fishermen are standing nearby, casts made with wide-sweeping movements can be hazardous. Make absolutely certain that there is

Fig. 179

no one standing or sitting anywhere near the path to be described by your casting movement. Relaxing your caution in this regard could result in the loss of an eye, or, at the very least, in a great deal of pain and inconvenience for some-one. Not to speak of a great deal of embarrass-ment for the careless angler.

More arm extension than normal and a swing-ing stroke that lofts the bait through a relatively high arc bring the cast to completion.

Swing the bait gently backward, stopping the rod tip at about one o'clock (Fig. 178).

Apply the power with a gentle, progressive squeeze of the grip (Fig. 179).

Fig. 180

Release the line at a very high point in the casting arc, about eleven-thirty (Fig. 180). Be extremely careful to note where your companions are located before making this sort of cast.

Fig. 181

Two-Handed Power Cast

Sometimes when fishing with subsurface lures and baits, like artificial plastic worms, very long retrieves are needed for adequate water coverage. The long retrieves, of course, necessitate some very long casts.

The easiest way to generate and store more energy in the rod in a fishing situation is with the two-handed power cast. The off hand grasps the butt of the handle throughout the movements and supplies much of the power.

The backstroke is made in the normal manner, but over a slightly longer arc (Figs. 181 and 182).

Fig. 182

Fig. 183

During a forward stroke, the rod hand serves as a hinge or fulcrum. Notice in Fig. 183 how the caster's hands are working in opposing directions to unleash a cast of tremendous velocity. Close-ups of the hand positions and movements will be shown in the following chapter on bait-casting.

Fig. 184

Fig. 185

Backhand Cast

Backhanded spinning casts have broad application, whether you're fishing from a boat with other anglers for companions, or solving the casting problems offered by small, brushy streams. The arc of the backhanded spinning strokes describes the same basic path over the shoulder as in fly-casting.

Here, Lew Jewett, of 3M's Liesure Time Products New Business Ventures Division, an excellent caster, demonstrates the correct technique on a top Midwestern smallmouth-bass stream.

The cast is begun just as in the basic overhead cast with a slight dipping of the rod tip, followed by the backcast stroke to the vertical position. This time, however, the rod is taken back across the opposing shoulder (Fig. 184). The remainder of the movements are the same as in the basic cast (Figs. 185, 186, and 187). However, since the cast is made in a semi-horizontal plane, the point of release is more difficult to ascertain. As a result, effective backhanded casting with spinning tackle requires a bit more practice than overhead casting.

Fig. 186

Fig. 187

Horizontal Casts

Casts made in the fully horizontal to semi-horizontal planes are among the most useful to the angler employing spinning tackle. They're needed for casting lures and baits under overhanging bushes as well as making lobbing casts with soft, fragile live or cured baits. However, they should not be used when others are in the vicinity of the casting arc.

The basic horizontal stroke is a very easy one, but accuracy is not one of the advantages of this mode of casting.

Snap the rod tip back to the side very briskly (Fig. 188), as in the overhead cast. Use wrist motion with a lure or tough artificial bait, a more gentle sweeping stroke with delicate natural baits. The forward stroke is made as in the overhead cast, but in the horizontal plane. You'll need to angle the strokes enough to get an arc appropriate to the required distance. Otherwise the lure or bait will hit the surface prematurely.

Fig. 188

Fig. 189. A 12-pound spinning-hooked steelhead takes to the air.

Other Casts

Two other casts are sometimes needed by spinning anglers. They are the bow-and-arrow cast and the flip cast. They are made precisely the same way with spinning tackle as they are with bait-casting and fly-casting equipment. The bow-and-arrow cast is described in Chapter 10.

Chapter 13

Casting with Bait-Casting Tackle

Assembling the Tackle

Bait-casting and spin-casting rods are so similar in design and the ways in which they're cast that both types of equipment are dealt with simultaneously in this chapter.

Bait-casting and spin-casting rods usually come in one- or two-piece versions with detachable handles. In assembling the rod, join the two rod sections together first, taking the usual care to line up the guides. Then, insert the butt section into the handle and affix the reel.

Some bait-casting handles have separate knurled rings with which to fasten down the reel. The mechanism which locks the handle to the rod butt (usually a collet) sometimes is designed to fasten down the reel at the same time.

Before attaching the reel to the handle, it should be filled to the proper level with bait-casting line (either flat mono or braided bait-casting line), which is normally about $1/16$ to $1/8$ inch below the top edge of the spool. Never overfill a bait-casting or spin-casting reel spool. Do not try to fill a spin-casting reel with braided casting line. Water accumulated by the braided line tends to build up in the small nose-cone hole and reduces the efficiency of the cast.

When rod and reel are correctly assembled, the line is strung through the guides, and a practice plug is affixed to the line, you're ready to start some practice casting.

But first you'll need to make a couple of reel adjustments peculiar to bait-casting reels.

Adjusting the Bait-Casting Reel

Notice that centered on each sideplate of the bait-casting reel is a knurled cap. On some reels both

of the caps can be turned. On others only one can be adjusted. The end caps, as they're called, permit centering the spool and adjusting the amount of play it has between the bearings. Turn one of the caps until the spool is centered. Then, after centering the spool precisely, adjust the other just to the point where lateral play is eliminated.

The reel's anti-backlash mechanism will also need an adjustment. Most modern-day bait-casting reels have such an adjustment to assist beginning casters in learning to cast without troublesome backlashes—the plague of the beginner's existence.

Most present-day reels have devices that can be set to put friction on the axle or otherwise respond to the centrifugal forces created by the revolving spool. The latter type is called a centrifugal brake by tackle makers. It consists of braking blocks that slide in and out on tiny rods mounted on the spool's axle. The braking blocks slide outward in response to the centrifugal force. When they reach the outer ends of the rods they create friction with a brake shoe—the faster the revolutions, the more the braking friction.

The most important thing to remember about any of the anti-backlash devices is that they are put there to aid the tyro caster in learning how to thumb the reel. Once he has mastered the delicate art of thumbing the bait-casting reel spool, he'll undoubtedly want to set the drag all the way off to enjoy the pleasure of effortless, long casting. Virtually all of the anti-backlash mechanisms reduce casting distance considerably.

Most of the best bait-casting reels manufactured today are made with anti-reverse handles that help prevent losing control of a heavy fish, star-drag mechanisms, and free-spooling buttons that disengage the spool from the gears to permit easy casting.

The most primitive early-day reels simply had a set of transfer gears that translated handle turns into spool rotation. Free-spooling casting reels came later. Some had level-wind mechanisms, others didn't. The star drags and anti-reverse handles are the most recent innovations.

Whichever type of bait-casting reel you own, adjusting the anti-backlash drag is really very easy. First assemble the rod, string it up, and attach a practice plug.

If it's one of the latest models, reel the plug close to the rod tip. Then, push in the free-spooling button. If the plug drops to the ground rapidly and the line tangles on the spool, more drag is needed. Tighten the adjustment a tiny bit at a time until the plug descends at a more moderate rate and no tangling results when it lands on the ground. As you become more proficient at the art of thumbing the reel you'll be able to gradually reduce the amount of drag until someday no drag at all will be required.

How to Grip the Bait-Casting Rod

Grasp the handle of the bait-casting rod as if you were going to shake hands with someone. Wrap the tip of your index finger comfortably around the triggerlike extension. Let your thumb fall naturally into place on the surface of the spooled line (Fig. 190). The reel handle should be on top, the spool in a vertical position so that it's resting directly on a single bearing. This reduces friction and makes possible some very long, effortless casts.

If the reel has a free-spooling mechanism and the handle an anti-reverse lock, these should be engaged until just before you make the cast.

The basic hand position is the same for the spin-casting reel (Fig. 191), the reel handle in the on-top position, thumb resting on the trigger. Make certain the trigger is in the locked position also until just prior to the cast.

From this point on, the casting techniques will be the same for both types of equipment, except for the method of releasing the line.

With the bait-casting reel, the thumb is held firmly on the spooled line throughout the casting strokes until the actual release. The thumb also "feathers" the spooled line as the casting weight shoots toward the target.

In the case of the spin-casting reel, the thumb depresses the trigger on the reel firmly throughout the casting strokes, releasing the pressure as the casting weight is sped on its way. If the caster wants to halt the lure during its flight to the target, he merely depresses the trigger again.

Fig. 190

Fig. 191

Basic Overhead Cast

The multiplying bait-casting reel provides maximum line control and accuracy for casting lures, plugs, weighted spinners, drift baits, and saltwater lures. Line control is more limited with spin-casting reels.

The basic cast is a wrist snap imparted in conjunction with a short, very firm lift of the forearm. Hold the upper arm relaxed but in control close to the body.

Grip the rod, positioning the thumb against the spooled line on the bait-casting reel or lightly on the trigger of the spin-casting reel, as in Figs. 190 and 191.

First, depress the free-spooling button on your bait-casting reel with your free hand, or the trigger of the spin-casting reel with the thumb of your casting hand. In both cases, make sure that you maintain good firm thumb pressure until releasing the lure at the end of the forward casting stroke.

Visually sight in on your target by raising the rod tip to a point over the target area (Fig. 192).

The secret of accurate casting is to establish a set order of executing the strokes—to "groove" the strokes in much the same way as the low-handicap golfer tries to groove his swing.

In bait-casting this is the way it's done. First, determine your own personal sighting points at the various distances. Depending on your eyesight and physical makeup, the sighting points may be variously dead center, right of center, or left of center as you look down the rod. Wind will also necessitate taking certain allowances.

The second important phase of the bait-casting stroke is to start the cast with a slight dipping of the rod tip. This resembles the golfer's "press" in that the backcast stroke flows directly from it. The rod-tip dip establishes the casting plane and loads the rod with a small amount of energy that assists in making a vigorous, positive backcast stroke. This dipping movement of the rod tip has a tendency to negate some of the acute, bilateral indecision many tyro casters have until they're certain of the basic rod strokes and how to manipulate their reels.

The timing of the bait-casting strokes is critically quick with the stiff worm and plug rods favored by many present-day anglers. Light-action fishing and tournament accuracy rods are somewhat slower in timing and, as a result, considerably easier to cast, resembling the action of a well-designed parabolic-action spinning rod.

After sighting in the cast, snap up the rod tip to the vertical position (Fig. 193), employing mostly

Fig. 192

wrist action and a slight forearm lift, as demonstrated here by M/Sgt. Thomas Stouffer, USAF (ret.), one of the top casting instructors in the country.

Begin the movement smoothly out of the dipping movement mentioned earlier. When casting with the the stiff-action rods, you'll soon discover

Fig. 193

there's virtually no time to pause at the top of the backcast before the rod becomes fully loaded with casting weight. With the stiffer rods, the forward movement flows directly out of the backcast (Fig. 194).

Stop the forward cast abruptly at a point between ten and eleven o'clock, releasing your thumb pressure altogether momentarily. You'll undoubtedly experience a few bad backlashes

until you discover precisely when to start feathering the spool with the thumb. When the lure hits the water, stop the spool instantly with firm thumb pressure.

In Figs. 196 through 200, Lew Jewett demonstrates the complete overhead cast made in an actual fishing situation on a smallmouth bass river. The strokes are precisely the same when a spin-cast reel is used.

Fig. 194

Fig. 195.   Smallmouth bass, an ideal fish on light bait-casting tackle.

Fig. 196.   Start cast with a slight dip of the rod tip.

Fig. 197.   Backcast flows directly out of the dipping movement.

Fig. 198.   Rapidly accelerated wrist-snap starts the backcast.

Fig. 199.   Forward stroke is a wrist-snap to between ten and eleven o'clock.

Fig. 200.   Lure is released—rod tip allowed to follow through.

Fig. 201.   Bait-casting is ideal for stump-choked water like this.

Fig. 202

Power Cast

Long-range fishing casts with bait-casting rods can be made in both the vertical and the horizontal planes. The basic rod strokes are the same as in the overhead cast. But this time, both hands are used to apply more leverage to the rod—to bend it more and store up additional energy, as in any two-handed cast.

The caster sights in over the rod tip. Note that his left hand rests lightly on the handle butt (Fig. 202).

The rod tip is snapped up into the backcast stroke with considerable speed (Fig. 203).

Fig. 203

Fig. 204

The rod tip is snapped forward, the free hand imparting additional leverage and the casting hand acting as a fulcrum point (Fig. 204).

Fig. 205

Backhand Cast

Backhanded casting with a bait-casting rod adapts to the same angling purposes as with backhanded fly-casting and spinning. However, because of the very quick timing of the fishing rods in current use, the cast isn't easy and takes considerable practice. Once learned it becomes an indispensable boon when you are fishing from boats and in proximity to other anglers, who might be endangered by an ordinary cast.

At the start of the cast, the sighting-in, hand, arm, and rod positions are identical to those used in the overhead cast (Fig. 205).

Fig. 206

However, this time, the backcast wrist snap carries the rod back over your opposing shoulder (Fig. 206).

The delivery is as in the overhead cast, directed to the sight-in point and released between ten and eleven o'clock (Fig. 207).

Figs. 208 to 211 show the cast being made in an angling situation with a spin-casting reel.

Fig. 207

Fig. 208.   Cast begins with the sighting-in and rod-tip dip . . .

Fig. 209.   . . . out of which the backcast flows smoothly.

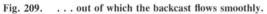

Fig. 210.   Rod is snapped back over opposing shoulder with wrist movement . . .

Fig. 211.   . . . then forward to eleven-o'clock position, where plug is released.

Fig. 212

Horizontal Cast

Although the horizontal cast is by far the easiest of the bait-casting casts, it certainly isn't the most accurate and is not recommended when fishing in close proximity to other anglers. The cast is used when it is necessary to fire a cast under overhanging tree limbs and bushes, and when making long-distance exploratory casts in fairly open water.

The rod strokes (Figs. 212 to 215) are exactly the same as those for the horizontal spinning cast.

Fig. 213

Fig. 214.   The horizontal release.

Fig. 215.   The rod tip follows through toward the target.

Fig. 216. Larry Dahlberg spots a likely-looking pocket under an overhanging tree branch.

Fig. 217. Backward stroke is short, highly compressed. Casting movement is mostly wrist-snap.

Flip Cast

Flip-casting with spinning, spin-casting, and bait-casting rods is a highly useful but somewhat tricky maneuver used to shoot a cast lure under overhanging brush or tree limbs. It can be accomplished in one of two ways, either with vertical or horizontal rod movements. The cast is most often used when angling from a boat, and occasionally when wading in a stream. The backhanded technique in the semi-horizontal plane is illustrated here.

The flip-cast is essentially nothing more than a backhanded cast in which the strokes are dramatically compressed.

In this version of the cast, where a spin-casting rod and reel are demonstrated, the cast is begun with the rod tip held within 18 inches of the water, the rod itself angled diagonally across the body to avoid striking the boat handler and an angling companion (Fig. 216).

As I mentioned before, the stroke is made in a highly compressed manner, the rod tip being snapped sharply back a foot or two, the forward stroke consisting of a backhanded "flip" of the rod tip (Figs. 217 and 218).

Flip-casting may also be accomplished with vertically aligned rod strokes. When this plane is selected, the rod tip is sighted in in the usual fashion over the target area. Then, the tip is snapped straight down, the forward flip being imparted in an upward direction. The method is easily adapted to spinning tackle as well; the basic strokes are exactly the same.

Fig. 218. Lure travels a very flat trajectory to target area.

Bow-and-Arrow Cast

The bow-and-arrow cast is one of the most useful of the specialty casts to the angler fishing brush-bordered small streams and obstruction-choked lakes and impoundments. Its purpose, of course, is to shoot a plug, bait, or lure into a highly restricted pocket. At best, it is a short-range cast that permits pinpoint accuracy in tight quarters where a backcast may be impossible.

The cast is begun by grasping the plug at the bend of the trailing hooks. If you grasp the more forward-placed hooks, you risk implanting the trailing hooks in your fingers at the release. The casting weight is dropped down from the rod tip on a length of line about one-half that of the rod itself, then pulled back far enough to put enough bend in the rod to load it fully with energy.

Aim the rod directly at the target area, then release the held plug or lure (Figs. 219 and 220).

The lure will be propelled in a straight cast directly toward the target, provided the caster does not impart any movement to the rod up through the release of the lure.

Fig. 220   **Fig. 219**

Chapter 14

Surf-Casting

Assembling the Tackle

Two-handed surf-casting rods and their matching spinning or bait-casting reels are assembled just like their one-handed freshwater counterparts.

The main differences between surf-casting reels of both types and their freshwater equivalents are their larger size, their greater durability and strength of construction, and the noncorrosive metals from which they're fashioned.

By far the most popular type of bait-casting reel for casting in surf conditions is the "squidder," as anglers normally refer to it. It is simply a multiplying, star-drag bait-casting reel of larger size, and usually features a free-spooling mechanism. But most modern surfcasters use spinning gear.

Spinning surf-casters are showing increasing interest in saltwater reels of the "skirted spool" type. In this reel the flange of the spool wraps around the gear and shaft housing, thus preventing line from being blown into the housing and any resulting tangles.

Fig. 221. **A heavy bait-casting reel for surf-casting.**

Fig. 222

Fig. 223

Gripping the Rod

With both types of reel, the left hand grasps the butt of the long handle, in the case of a right-handed caster. The right hand controls the bait-casting reel in exactly the same way as in single-handed casting, the thumb feathering the rotating spool as the lure sails out toward the target. When the lure lands in the water, the thumb exerts full pressure on the spool to prevent it from overrunning (Figs. 221 and 222).

With a saltwater spinning reel, the right-hand grip is precisely the same as with a single-handed rod (Fig. 223). In the casting sequences to follow, reels of both types will at times be shown within the same sequence. This is done to point up the fact that the casting strokes are precisely the same, regardless of the kind of reel being used.

The caster in these photos is Mr. Gil Hokanson, of Los Angeles, California, one of the West Coast's most prominent anglers and tournament casters.

Soft-Bait Cast

Although the average freshwater angler pictures the typical surf-caster as one who propels the lure or bait with a mighty overhead casting motion, normally referred to as the "figure-8" cast, a considerable amount of serious surf fishing is done with soft baits like shrimps and softshell crabs that would be ripped from the hooks by the force of such rod strokes.

As a result, many of the more knowledgeable surf-casters start this cast by laying the baits and casting sinker fully extended by a rod length or more on the sand behind them (Fig. 224).

The angler assumes a stance with the rod held parallel to the water behind him, enough tension on the line to lift the soft baits clear of the abrasive sand (Fig. 225). At this stage of the cast, the caster's weight is distributed toward the right foot. His arms are well extended and parallel to the water.

The forward stroke is accomplished by a very smooth sweeping movement of the rod through a vertical or near-vertical arc (Fig. 226). The right-hand movement is forward, the hand serving as the fulcrum of the lever (rod). The left hand, which is grasping the butt of the handle, imparts

Fig. 224

Fig. 225

Fig. 226

Fig. 227

counterforce back toward the angler's body. The angler's body weight smoothly shifts from the right to the left foot during this movement (Fig. 227), and great power is lent to the cast by the turning shoulders.

Fig. 228 shows the caster in the classic position of the release, which allows the line to flow smoothly through the guides, instead of against them. Fig. 229 illustrates the rod position at the time of lure impact with the water.

Fig. 228

Fig. 229

Fig. 230

Basic Surf Cast

Balance and weight shift are extremely important in long-distance surf-casting. The position of the feet at the start of the cast is approximately the same as for distance fly-casting, only a bit more spread. The left side of the right-handed caster's body faces the target area. The left foot is firmly planted in the sand, well in advance of the right. During the lift and back stroke the weight shifts to the right foot. The forward stroke starts with a shifting of the body weight to the left foot (Fig. 230), rather like the weight shift in the golf swing. As the caster drives forward, turning his shoul-

Fig. 231.   The backcast stroke is begun with a lift of the rod tip and a body turn to the right.

ders into the forward stroke, the left leg acts as a pivot point, permitting the full body and shoulder turn that delivers energy to the rod.

The caster must be adaptable to unfavorable conditions of wind, undertow, and surf. And when they occur, as in the sequence to follow, he may be forced to sacrifice a little distance by assuming a stance that permits him to maintain his balance. Figs. 231 to 238 illustrate such a situation—forceful, gusting winds, a hard-running incoming tide from north to south (right to left), and a steeply inclined beach where undertow created highly unstable footing.

In this situation the usual foot position was abandoned in favor of balance. You will find other adjustments necessary in other situations.

Fig. 232.   The lifting movement is continued vertically, with the shoulders also turning into the stroke.

Fig. 233.   Here, the casting weight swings past the caster's head on the backward stroke.

Fig. 234.   The rod nears the completion of the back stroke. Note the full extension of the left arm and how the right hand cradles the weight of the rod.

Fig. 235.   Begin the forward casting stroke with a pushing movement of the right hand and a backward pulling with the left.

Fig. 236.   After the energy of the stroke has been released at approximately eleven o'clock, the rod tip snaps down below the point of release, and then . . .

Fig. 237. . . . returns to the point where the release of the casting weight was made.

Fig. 238.   A closeup of the same rod position shown in Fig. 237, except that the caster is using a "squidder" type of bait-casting reel.

Index